The Quiet in the Land

A Volga-German's Christian Journals:
Russian Revolution Years 1916-1918

Henry P. Wieler

Edited and Abridged by
Arthur L. Pavlatos and
Michael C. Upton

"To be spiritually rich means to have earthly modesty.

To be earthly rich means to have spiritual need."

– Brother Sturm, 1918

A special thank you to my wife, Mary Jane, who supported
me in this effort and gave much of her time to the project.

Arthur L. Pavlatos

© Copyright 2005 Arthur L. Pavlatos.
All rights reserved. No part of this publication may be reproduced, stored in a retrieval
system, or transmitted, in any form or by any means, electronic, mechanical, photocopying,
recording, or otherwise, without the written prior permission of the author.

*Cover design by Arthur L. Pavlatos's daughter, Georgina (Gina) L. Donnelly
Photography by Brian R. Donnelly
Page Layout and Design by Sombodies Productions, New Holland, PA 17555*

Note for Librarians: a cataloguing record for this book that includes Dewey Decimal
Classification and US Library of Congress numbers is available from the Library and
Archives of Canada. The complete cataloguing record can be obtained from their online
database at:
www.collectionscanada.ca/amicus/index-e.html
ISBN 1-4120-4786-2
Printed in Victoria, BC, Canada

TRAFFORD

Offices in Canada, USA, Ireland, UK and Spain
This book was published *on-demand* in cooperation with Trafford Publishing. On-demand
publishing is a unique process and service of making a book available for retail sale to the
public taking advantage of on-demand manufacturing and Internet marketing. On-demand
publishing includes promotions, retail sales, manufacturing, order fulfilment, accounting and
collecting royalties on behalf of the author.
Book sales for North America and international:
Trafford Publishing, 6E–2333 Government St.,
Victoria, BC V8T 4P4 CANADA
phone 250 383 6864 (toll-free 1 888 232 4444)
fax 250 383 6804; email to orders@trafford.com
Book sales in Europe:
Trafford Publishing (UK) Ltd., Enterprise House, Wistaston Road Business Centre,
Wistaston Road, Crewe, Cheshire CW2 7RP UNITED KINGDOM
phone 01270 251 396 (local rate 0845 230 9601)
facsimile 01270 254 983; orders.uk@trafford.com
Order online at:
www.trafford.com/robots/04-2594.html

10 9 8 7 6 5 4 3

Contents

	Page
Table of Religious Contents	4
Introduction	5

CHAPTER 1 - 1916
Take a Moment	10
Of German Christians, World War I, and the World	13
Death in Winter	19

CHAPTER 2 - 1917
The Relationship of the Human Soul to the Creator	22
Time for Prayer and Reflection	27
Thanksgiving Services	30
Braun's Sermon	36
Two Sermons	40
The Coming of the Holidays	45

CHAPTER 3 - WINTER 1918
Prayers for Health, Friendship and Deliverance	50
The Siberian Baptists	58
The Conference Evening Service	67
A Harvest Sermon	70
Hammer's Sermon	72
Lessons from the Lord	87
Notes from the Past	96

CHAPTER 4 - SPRING 1918
The Last Months in Siberia	100
The Journey Home and a Story	110

Appendix A	115
Appendix B	116
Epilogue	123

Religious Contents

	Page
Temptation	32
Denial	33
Jesus' Mission	34
Jesus' Coming	38
The Redeemer	40
Repentance	42
Christmas Program	45
Paying Debts	50
The Last Hour	52
The Conference	53
Fellowship	54
God's Workers	54
The Siberian Baptists	57
The End is Near	67
The Harvest Sermon	69
Coming Salvation	72
The True Grapevine	79
The Bouquet	82
Two Sermons	87
House of Faith	88
Paul's Confession	89
God Locked Up	89
God's Music	90
To Be Helped	92
"That Ye Put Off"	97
Cleanse Us	97
What To Do	101
Sin	102
The Holy Spirit	104
Baptism	105
Greta	105
Storm and Change	111

Introduction

The journals of Henry P. Wieler were tucked away, shielded from time, stowed in the darkness of a small garden shed for years. Covered in dust, the ornate ledgers were left to rest alone, but had not been forgotten. It was Harry Wieler, son of Henry Wieler, who first brought the journals to light in 1992. A special thank you is issued to Harry who had enough faith in this project to share photographs, archives, and recollections of his father and family.

This book, a compilation of spiritual writings found in the journals, begins in 1916. The handwritten entries in the journals of Henry Wieler start several years before 1916, but few are wrapped with such strong religious language as the years of 1916-1918. Wieler shares with the reader a spiritual journey as he takes time from his busy life to record his innermost thoughts.

The religious writings herein contained are a reflection of Wieler's search for Christian understanding—his attempt to live a religious life during troubled times. For all of his life, Henry was affiliated with the Anabaptist, Mennonite, and Baptist Christian traditions. In the early twentieth century, practitioners of these religious values, along with the Lutheran & Catholic Christian churches, were granted special existence in Russia. These religious groups formed strong German speaking communities in a foreign and soon changing Russia. It was Tsar Catherine the Great who invited the industrious, land working Germans into Russia in order to help farm the fertile regions of her country. In the early twentieth century, there were over 1 million ethnic German people living in Russia, most along the Volga River. The German Christians were great stewards of the land and produced abundant crops for the benefit of all Russia. Still, they were "German-Russians, the Quiet in the Land," and watched over by a different eye than that which saw over the rest of the Russian population.

Wieler, finding himself in Siberia teaching at German schools, learns more of God and His teachings than he expected. While his love of the Lord grew, his love of his profession and surroundings waned. The world became engulfed in the conflict later to be known as World War I. At this busy time in his life, Wieler knows both the joy of fatherhood and the despair of uncertainty. There are words to describe what he felt and he placed them masterfully onto paper—in German.

Translations were needed to evaluate the content of the "rediscovered," original manuscripts. After many local translation efforts were unsuccessful, Bert Friesen of Winnipeg, Manitoba, Canada, completed what has become the first phase in a project that sheds light on an invaluable firsthand historical resource. These are the years 1916 through 1918. Mr. Friesen, fluent in German, resides in an area where many early European Christians immigrated.

The results of this initial translation were exciting. Henry wrote freely and explicitly, not only about his everyday life, but also about his Christian being. He reflected on the Bible and its specific verses and teachings. Wieler recorded church sermons and landmark religious conferences. These are often paraphrased after the occasion with skill that seems almost verbatim. Through these recordings we are privy to the religious events and services of the time. (Double indented sections of this book are the paraphrased conversations of the speaker/preacher. This indentation serves notice to the reader while attempting to retain the tone or structure of the original entries.)

Besides being focused on a truly Christian life, Henry was a versatile man taking up photography and other artistry. He was often commissioned to paint decorative plaques that were over written with scripture or moral verses. These are referred to as "wall sayings" in Wieler's journals. This artistry became a livelihood later in the United States. Wieler also sang in the church choir and played the harmonium.

His wife, Suse, was a midwife and bonesetter and practiced her profession throughout the region. She suffered with several illnesses while raising a family in rural, southern Siberia.

In total there are five journals, varying in length and girth, all nearly equivalent to an accountants ledger. The paper is old and fading, yet in remarkable condition for its age. The ink, a sometimes precious substance, resonates from the page. The script is ornate and decorative, itself taking the reader on as much a journey as the words do weave. Over fifteen hundred pages are accumulated in these rare capsules of life. A reader of all five journals will travel back to the birth of Henry Wieler in 1891 up to the year 1924, when he arrived in the United States.

Some parts are lost forever. Time has taken its toll on the journals of Henry Wieler, as it does on all history of man. Months, sometimes years, are missing from Wieler's recordings.

With creative assistance from Michael C. Upton, compilation and editing was completed in late 2004. Now, the Christian writings from the journals of Henry Wieler are available for all to share.

Wieler's writing shows him searching for a true understanding of the Christian life while the world around him was spinning in turmoil. Through his writing he reaches out and asks for God's help to guide him and his family along a path that is truly Christian.

The years of 1916 through 1918 hold much more: war and politics, profession and society, but it is the word of God that most touched Henry Wieler. These are his words...

Editors note: Narrative paragraphs have been inserted in order to give the reader a cleaner understanding of the timeline of the journals. Wieler wrote of many events happening in his life, some of these items, not relevant to Christian discussion, have been omitted from the book. The narrative paragraphs have been included to inform the reader of any substantial circumstances not mentioned or fully explained in the provided text. These narrative paragraphs are set in italic font.

Additionally, Appendices have been placed at the end of the book which may shed further light on historical and biographical information.

Russia 1917

 Volga - German Settlements

The five original journals
1912-1924

1916

Ein neues Jahr! Wir stehen stille;
Herzen stürmen brausend Fragen;
und Blumen Deutschland möge
sich schon nur stiftete sorgen!
…
…
…
…

1916

Take a Moment

We start in January; Wieler takes time to record a lengthy entry concerning the teachings and wisdom of God. During the winter of 1916 he writes of little else. His everyday reflections turn to meditation. He begins to write as a means of therapy, to discuss on paper the questions of religion that arise within him.

January 1916

The wind of a fierce storm, which roars through the forests, splinters hundred year old oak trees and uproots the tallest fir trees. The wind disturbs the sea so it sends its spray to the heavens; the sea toys with the steel reinforced war ships at the docks. The wind is praise of God and a voice of the Almighty. Just as the rolling thunder echoes through the land, so does the voice of the almighty, speaking earnestly to the hearts of men about the omnipotence of the Creator and preaches that we are but dust and His creation.

But, no less than the storm do the tiny rays of sunlight which entice the cold Earth to Spring show the praises of the Lord. The gentle spring breezes, which rustle the new leaves of the birch trees, the blooming lime trees which bring such sweet odors, and the newly hatched butterflies flying on their virgin wings, are all praises of God. As some preach about God's power and might, so others preach about his love and friendship.

The number of God's messengers is endless, as unmeasurable as his creation, the Universe—their shape as inexhaustible and varied as nature itself. Exalted and strong, rough and powerful, loving and gentle, so come the angels of God to us as His voice. What the angels make known cannot be contradicted, and to the unpracticed ear their words may disappear. The angels' tones may ring: harmonizing in wonderful chords and melodies to create a beautiful and glorious concert. They proclaim the will of the one and only Lord.

That same breeze, which today in a gentler manner cools our cheeks, can tomorrow become a mighty hurricane and throw us to the ground. If there were no storms in the air or on the sea, the air and the sea would grow dissolute and the creatures that lived in them would get sick. The same lightning that strikes fear from the thunderclouds also cleans the air and refreshes all earthly inhabitants with renewed vigor. God could not be the all-benevolent if he was not also the omnipotent Lord of Creation. The same sun which scorches and burns the tropical lands, also helps the palm trees grow heavenward and gently ripens the bananas and sugarcane. The same fire that may turn all our goods and chattels to ashes is also the power that creates human life—without it people would be like the beasts in the forest.

Everything, wherever you look and whatever you touch, everything serves the Great One, the incomparable Eternal One: Your God!

This God, the Creator of the entire universe, the creator of the giant animals before the Noahic flood, the preserver of all life and manager of everything that moves, is our God who guides our fate by his pleasure.

Do we live in peace, like the stream of water by his righteousness, like the rhythmic waves of the sea? Deep peace! Clear Flood! All of His righteousness overcoming might, and are we peaceful? On the contrary!

How confusing our life is to us. Like the pounding in a machine shop, or the rush of a waterfall, so often is our life. Even if our outward life resembles a quiet path in the desert where no one can disturb our absolute serenity, it is not so. It is often in our lives that we acquire unrest; worries of all kinds, small and insignificant or large and tedious, attach to our being. Duties drive us from one unrest to the other as a hunter drives his prey. A multitude of questions disturb our spirit, so often we do not know how to respond. Plans, wishes, and goals besiege our heart, as an enemy might besiege a fortress. The agitations of life shakes in us as the leaves of the trees when the wind plays with them!

That is not all there is to life! Add to our life the colorful disturbances of a spiritual life, often the consequences of outward happenings. There are also inner struggles and shadows that are only evident through their consequences. Most of these consequences go unnoticed by our friends and family; we often do not allow them to see. Many things, big and small, trouble our tranquility and disturb our piece of mind.

But as it says . . . your piece would be like a stream of water and your righteousness like the sea!

How are we to attain it? How are we to reach this goal?

The scriptures hold the answer; they have set the conditions to which you can attain your peace, which you thought, unattainable. The condition is: O, that you observed my commands!

That is it!

Observe His commands! And His commands are not difficult!

Of German Christians, World War I, and the World

In an attempt to capture the historical significance of his place in time, Wieler slips into a discussion that asks the direction of the German Christian people in this new world. He openly worries about the effects World War I will have on their way of life. During this time, Wieler discusses The Charter of Privileges, a provision allowing certain rights to these German Christians confirmed in 1800 by Tsar Paul I. The Charter was first established by Tsarina Catherine The Great in 1762 as an invitation to move to Russia.

Wieler fears his people's exile. It is in this section we first hear of plans to leave Russia. History shows that the majority of Volga region German Christians relocated to North America.

March

We live in a serious time!

Often, when remembering the events of our lifetime one might say, "It is a privilege to live in this time." Should one not consider those fortunate ones who do not have to experience our time?

In spite of the clouds that rise heavenward in our future and want to darken the sun; in spite of the uncertain future we face; in spite of all the injustice we face and which we might have to face; in spite of all the indifference and inertness happening in our spiritual lives; in spite of all this I believe it is a privilege to live in this time. It is a privilege, but also a great responsibility. There is but one thing I would ask from the Lord, one thing that I greatly desire. I ask that in this historic time we should be faithful to the One who bought us with His blood.

O God, accept me by Your grace and teach me through Your Word and Your spirit to observe Your commands! May I not only observe, but also help to keep them.

That is how it happens. I wanted to write down my feelings, but not exactly in this way. My goal was to enlighten about this time in history, and God is enlightening me by his light in my heart.

It is at the same time a serious and wonderful time in history! We live in a dangerous time, black clouds tower ominously in the sky. For nearly two years a disastrous war has been raging and demanding daily sacrifices. Blood flows in the streams and on the battlefields. People of various nations and faiths fill the Earth with the bones of their dead. In wartime they are enemies, in death they lie side by side and await the great resurrection morning. Daily we discover more gruesome ways in which people are sent into the beyond.

In our inner spiritual kingdom, away from the wild slaughter, do we have peace there? From a distance, we must believe not. Sickness, sin, and injustice disturbs the hearts of all. The suffering, which always follows such conflagrations, smirks at us from all corners of the Czar's empire. And the future holds no end in sight. The further into the future one imagines, the worse it must and will become! Darkness, nothing good, is the future; we are promised only terror and suffering.

As a people, we are a tiny population of Russia, and there is little hope in our future. There are storm clouds gathering on the horizon for our people. One does not have to step into an observatory to see that our stars are paling and will soon be falling. For a long time we counted on the blessings of our forefathers and believed in our security. O, the German Christians! How much good they have brought mankind! It is self-evident that God in Heaven is pleased with the German Christians and has richly blessed them. Who will confirm this?

Psalm 2:4

The German Christian people were protected from infringement until now. The confidence of our religion was built by our forefathers, and the reasoning that has built this solid entrenchment is being threatened. With horror, we can see through the walls. The foundations are damaged. Soon the enemy will be able to breach them and then the whole of our work will be destroyed.

The enemy can come!

Who is our enemy? Who is so hostile-minded against us, "the quiet in the land?" Who would want to destroy our good privileges? Is the enemy even strong enough to harm us? The law protects us! The Charter of Privileges which was granted our forefathers cannot be infringed upon now!

We should be safe, even if it is newly promulgated, to force us, as "Germans," from this country. From the highest circles of society it rings out to us below that the "Germans" should leave this country as their forefathers came. Should land and bread be taken away from us, and no country given to accept us? This country is at war not only with the Germans, but with everything German. Therefore, everything that is German, everything that speaks German and sounds German, must leave this country! That is the disposition.

We have been provoked! We have been wronged! We, the faithful subjects of His Majesty the Czar of all Russians, will be so badly handled. We feel deeply vexed that so little attention is paid to the good we have done. The empire has benefited from the contributions of the German Christian's for a long time.

It might be true that the emigration of Germans is a step backward for Russia, it is also a step backward for civilization. What is now the granary of the empire will likely loose its title if we are gone. The German cultivates his land more productively than the natives of this country. But, some ask, what else are we good for? They ask, what are our other "good" works?

Are we still "the quiet in the land?" Do we still have what our forefathers strived to obtain, that which is entailed in the title "the quiet in the land?" Often, are we not like the geese being driven to market by the farmer and his long rod? They were provoked by this slanderous treatment and spoke out against it. How did they get the idea to be so angry?

Our ancestors worshipped Rome! So it was! That is what our ancestors did, but what did you do? What value does it have for us?

Our actions and dealings here on Earth have probably provoked the Lord in Heaven to laugh and deride us. It is probably out of his hand that all this lightning from the dark clouds of the company of peoples is striking down and will hit us as well. Therefore, we have no reason to be disturbed about the injustice that has befallen us. Maybe it would be better if we would submit and say, "We need it Lord, Strike us!" Psalm 59:8.

It is a serious time. How it will finally turn out for the Germans in Russia cannot be predicted. The news that reaches us varies, and most of it may be only gossip and idle talk.

New Zealand and China, Japan and Canada will be considered as our future homes. Frenchmen and Englishmen, Tartars and Germans pass a rumor on to their own people that they want to accept us.

One thing is for sure, the needle on our scale continues back and forth. Only God knows where the needle will finally rest. Only He knows when the mighty of this world will speak the last word in regard to our future. He knows it and He rules the World! How fortunate!

We have tried many things in order to help the almighty Creator apply the right thing for our future. A deputation has been sent to the Czar to apply for mercy on our behalf. We are not depending on any rights or privileges, only mercy. On the other hand, it is rumored that the German parliament has decided to accept us as immigrants.

It is even whispered that the president of our Forest Service Organization has traveled to America in order to work something out in the United States. What is being worked out is not known. In Canada, it is said that a society has been formed which has purchased a large piece of land for a German Christian settlement. A delegation has been sent to Petrograd in order to gain permission for us to leave. The government has not yet granted permission.

Etc., etc.! In short, an effort is being made everywhere and the rumors travel unbelievably quick. How good is it to know, in this moving time, our life is not in the hands of men, but that everything hinges on the will of the Almighty Lord. Only this knowledge, and the calling to his arms, makes us happy and calm. Blessed, double blessed, are those who belong to Him.

After these entries, Wieler records mostly everyday events like the coming of Spring and the regular happenings of his school. In the Summer of 1916 (April 15 through August 15) Wieler returns to Pleshanovo and Alexandertal Colonies on vacation. His journal picks up again in September when Wieler records "after the fact out of memory" the people and places he visited while on vacation.

During this trip, his wife Suse, who was pregnant with the couples second child, became ill and was considered near death. Friends, relatives, and local doctors recommended that Suse have an operation to find the cause of the illness. Wieler records from memory searching for a surgeon and having to travel to the city in order to have the operation performed on his ailing wife. The operation, deemed successful, found no illness. This fact greatly worried the couple, the surgeon could give no medical explanation for the pains. Suse spent several days recovering from surgery. While still recovering, Suse reported having pains of a different nature. She was only five months pregnant and the hospital dismissed her claim that she may be going into labor. The couple insisted on seeing a doctor or midwife, but neither made an appearance. Wieler describes the events of May 23, 1916: At 9 o'clock in the morning she gave birth. When finally a supervisory nurse came, and in typical Russian calmness, asked if she really had genuine labor contractions, I could answer her : "No, she does not have any labor pains, she has given birth!"

On this vacation Wieler learned the art of photography and began to master the skill of photographic processing through the instruction of a friend in Neu Samara Colony. While in Neu Samara he purchased a camera and all the necessary accessories from a mutual friend who was returning to active military service and had no need of the equipment. Photography later became a valuable source of income for the Wieler household.

Death in Winter

In the winter months of 1916, Wieler seldom writes in his journals. Often he takes opportunity on Sundays or Holidays to catch up on the prior weeks events. During this time many deaths befall the community and friends of the Wieler's, he records these events without hesitation.

In November, Wieler mentions the fact that he is making a "wall plaque." Original translations describe these items as: "wall sayings (wall plaque with a saying)." Wieler was quite artistic with his calligraphy and was often commissioned to create decorative plaques with biblical verses. This artistry, like photography, in time becomes a valuable source of extra income for the family.

October 24, 1916
"There, under the green fields in Asia, under the wall of Erzerums, the cool Earth covers the body of our beloved brother Peter." That is what Brother Heinrich Tows wrote on the 14th of this month in a letter we have just received. Peter's wife contributed a few lines also, and reported the death of Gustav Janzen along with her husband.

We are deeply moved when we receive news of the death of loved ones. The messenger, whom God sends to us, their duty is to call to us: Remember! Be mindful of death! O, God! Teach us to reflect upon ourselves and accept the fact that we must die.

November 6, 1916

Snow! White on white!

The snow today blanketed the land in a light dusting, now this evening it is a heavy snowfall. Content is he who is at home beside the warm oven and can enjoy himself there.

Today there was a funeral in Nikolaifeld; we were invited. Mrs. Wiebe died after struggling with a lengthy illness. We could not be there because no one took us along.

We have begun the day with new intentions. We intend to hold evening devotion services. For a long time we had neglected our evening worship. The fact that it has come to this point is a disgrace. It only shows that if my faith were measured by the thermometer, that thermometer would almost read zero!

I am the guilty one. It was my responsibility as minister of my house church to be mindful of such things. O, Father in Heaven, forgive me! Forgive your abnormal child who is only a disgrace and pain to you through life! I am only worthy of being cast off from you. Too much of your kindness, patience, and gentle heart have been used up on me! O, God! Take me on and help me to search for You more diligently in your Word.

Lord, thanks be to you for the varied help to get through this Autumn! Forgive my unfriendly behavior towards my family, which is a direct result of my estrangement from you. Help me out of the labyrinth of my remoteness from God into which I have strayed! You, Lord, I trust! You are to be my One and All!

November 8, 1916

Yesterday at 10 o'clock in the evening Suse was called for. Her services as a midwife and bonesetter were needed in Alexanderkron, but still today she has not returned.

Today winter has arrived. A heavy frost ensures us that the snow will stay, snow which has fallen continually over the last month.

After an hour, Suse returned home, and again she is gone. For this new trip, I suppose she has been engaged as a midwife.

Today we received a funeral invitation. The old Mr. Jacob Regier is to be buried on the tenth of this month.

November 19, 1916

I did not get around to writing this past week; I have had too much to do. On Sunday, we sat quietly at home. In the morning, I again was in church, where David Nickel spoke for the first time. He was commissioned many years ago as a preacher, and now after completing his national service; he has decided to take up his calling.

Monday was a national holiday and we had no school. I busied myself making a wall plaque that was ordered some time ago. Suse busied herself with her many patients, she even called upon a patient at their home.

As evening approached, a carriage suddenly arrived from Alexanderkron to get me. Johann Friesen's sons drove the carriage and informed me that Mr. Epp, from Andreasfeld, had arrived at their home for a brief visit. When we arrived, I found many colleagues and friends there.

I was disappointed that Mr. Epp could not tell me anything about Suse's or my parents. Still, there was much news imparted that evening. Most of the conversation was about the war and the banditry that is raging in the south. Two deaths were talked about which were of great importance to me.

On November 1st a teacher from Ohrloff died, Johann Braul. A great man has departed from our midst. For me he was more than just a teacher and great man. But, the Ohrloff Secondary School has become an orphan, its father has been lost. Was he saved when he died? God grant it! I would gladly see him again!

We also talked about the fact that on November 8th the Austrian Emperor, the 86 year-old sovereign ruler of such varied ethnic races jumbled into one empire, died. His nephew, the young Karl Franz Joseph has replaced him.

November 27, 1916

Our Wilhelm arrived with one of his colleagues in the national service.

The old Mr. Heinrich Epp, who lived in Andreasfeld and whose wife is buried in the cemetery there, has died.

1797

Das Verhältnis der Mensch[en] zum [...]

1917

The Relationship of the Human Soul to the Creator

In 1917 The Revolution came. Wieler, busy with teaching and at the same time worried about the future (as were many) had little time to compose journal entries. Most of the later entries deal with school starting and are filled with reflections of things that happened over the summer. During the summer months, Wieler vacationed in Alexandrowka, spending time with family and friends.

Before summer can grow vacations with family, the chill of Siberian winter forces him to contemplate the relationship between man and God.

Let me recall the use of the ancient hospitality.
Before one parted company with his guests, the head of the household broke a tonal receptacle at a precise point and gave the guest one half while the host kept the other. After many years, if the two broken pieces were brought together and joined, it would make possible a renewal of that hospitality.
The relationship between the human soul and its Creator is similar. His hand has put into the soul an abundance of abilities and talent. He has established in the soul moral sensibility and moral vitality. This, He himself, the living God, wants to see in all of us. God will see that "the human will be like Him." His picture rests on the deepest foundation and misguided longing moves the human soul until it looks up to Him and grasps his rays, his holy picture "reflects from one glory to another."

II. Cor. 3:18: But we all reflect, with open face, the glory of the Lord reluctantly and are changed into the same image, from glory to glory, even as by the Spirit of the Lord.

February 16, 1917

This week, which has gone by as quickly as the others, has brought me no work. I feel so useless. On Saturday I only had two photography jobs, which were not worthwhile enough for me to even take them. Now it seems that I have nothing to do.

The day before yesterday we had guests visit, brethren who conducted a service in my schoolroom. Brother Kröker, from Borodin, used as his text the words of Moses: "How He loves his people!" This love reaches all people, everyone can feel God's love. Brother Reimer, from Margenau, spoke of Lot's wife: "Hurry and save your soul." But what was most important to me was the emphasis Brother Reimer put on the words of the angels, "I can not do anything until you are saved." A prophetic word.

The world of today's Sodom will also be destroyed, but God can do nothing until the chosen ones have been removed. They will ascend to Him in Heaven! Everywhere there are prophets and there are no words without meaning in God's holy word!

In the west a dark wall of clouds is being pulled down to the Earth. There will be more snow tomorrow. In February, we have had a lot of snowstorms, these clouds billowing down. In the schoolroom there are two window sills completely covered by drifts. In the yard and garden are drifts like miniature mountains! On days without clouds, when the sun shines down, one is blinded by the clean, white snow. It is instinct that forces our eyes closed, shutting out the magnificent glistening and sparkling. White as snow! How sublime the thought! How high the goal! White as snow! How far is it to there! For human intentions and fulfilment an impossibility! But for the Creator of everything an only "to be!"

March 14, 1917

Yesterday we received the first newspapers published after the revolution. The old government was overthrown and a new one is now functioning. A lot of hard work has been done in the last few weeks, a lot was accomplished! The newspapers report that the 10th of March is to be designated as a National Holiday—remembrance of those who have fallen in the struggle for freedom.

However, I did not manage to read through all the news. I was absorbed in reading when unexpected guests made an appearance at our door. It was the engaged couple of Miss Penner and widower Abram Peters. We were informed that their wedding was to take place on the 21st of March. Only two months and ten days have passed since the funeral of Peters' first wife!

March 22, 1917

Today is my darling daughter Lilly's birthday. Two years have passed since she gave her first cry. Two years each with 365 days. These days have brought many new things to our family and those are only good things. It often seemed as if there was more bad than good, but it just seemed so. Again and again the good prevailed and one saw that everything came from the gracious Father's hand. O God, You are gracious!

In the afternoon I drove to the teacher's meeting in Margenau. A vote of confidence statement was prepared and signed. The final examinations were scheduled for April 11th and are to be conducted at our school. As I recall it, a final stipulation of agreement for the exams was that I should be present during their proctoring. Yes, the relationship between my colleagues and I is very curious.

Before we departed, Brother Hübert came and invited us all to a meeting of German Christians in the meeting house of the Alexandrowka General German Christian Church. (There were two main German Christian religious groupings in Russia: the General German Christians and the German Christian Brethren.) We, as teachers, decided to attend.

23 March 1917

Today we had our meeting in the church. Brother Hübert was voted as chairman, and Fröse and I as minute secretaries. To me, being voted minute secretary, was a big deal. I had never been a secretary in my life!

The purpose of the meeting was to form a committee to represent the concerns of the German Christians. We aimed to reflect the character of our people as representatives. Voted in by ballot were four persons, two teachers and two farmers. These delegates were to travel to Omsk for a meeting on the 9th of April.

April 2, 1917

Remember! Remember!

The joyous Easter days are here! The mysterious Maundy Thursday with its shady garden and dark foliage plays itself out with struggles and singing. The world does not remember those dried tears cried in deep quietude. Nor do they remember the gloomy Good Friday, crowds gathering as the cross was burdened through the streets. The world now does not hear the hammer blows, the spikes penetrating to the very marrow. The world now cannot see the three crosses pointing to heaven and sunk into the bloodstained earth. The world now does not know Good Friday with its heart-stifling darkness and the releasing and the departing of the redeemer. It is finished! The world does not understand the still Saturday with its so complete and definitely victorious grave and the important and serious guards looking into the grave and the shy followers, who had left his side, not far away.

All that is celebrated worthily or also unworthily; it is all thought proper or not proper.

Easter is here!

April 5, 1917

My old friend Friesen came for a 21-day holiday. After more than a year and a half of work, he is finally able to enjoy a holiday. It is good to see him and his family again. He is the same Friesen, just as he always was. In spiritual outlook Friesen is a windblown reed, fluctuating with the breeze. Pity about him!

April 11, 1917

Today was final examinations at the school. My students performed particularly well.

In the evening we visited the Friesen's where we celebrated the head of the household's birthday. When we arrived home we found a letter waiting with the most shattering news. Old Mr. Wiebe, who lived in the church house in Old-Samara, had ended his life on the 12th of March by suicide!

He had served the church for many years as a preacher, and now the enemy has made such an example of him.

God has spoken!

Who understands his difficult words?

Time for Prayer and Reflection

Sometime during the year, the Wieler's decided to relinquish their Siberian posts and move south, back toward the Volga region. Impeding their departure was the fact that Suse was pregnant with their second child.

During the summer months, Wieler recorded little in his actual journal. Instead, he jotted notes whenever the spirit moved him and later recorded the sometimes disjointed entries into his journal. Sometimes he wrote nothing down, remembering the importance of the events and latter retelling them in his journal. Often he followed these recordings with textual explanations and backward glances.

In July, Wieler was offered, and accepted a teaching position in Hoffnungstal. The new position finalized the families move from Alexandrowka, although they were not returning to the home colony of Alexandertal as originally planned.

From June 1917

There is much to do at home, yet we can think of nothing but moving back home to Pleshanovo Colony. We have packed and shipped the things we could do without. If Suse were not in the situation she is in, we would leave immediately. Now we must patiently wait until her term is completed and our family enlarged by a new member. Moving now would be difficult and would just make things worse for us, but we are anxious!

It was good that we had so much to do that summer. I traveled a lot between Moskalenki and Issil-Kulj, back and forth for various business reasons. At home, Suse had the pleasure and good companionship of Mrs. Langemann. I spent many nights in the train station alone. During these sleepless nights, I again made short entries for my journal, which I now insert. They seem to offer an explanation for the important changes happening to us.

July 24, 1917 (Issil-Kulj)
Gloomy and cold Autumn! The leaves are not yet falling, but the wind blows sorrowfully on and the summer will soon vanish!

God, the Lord, has again allowed us to experience that he is a Savior to man in his time of need. For a long, long time we have waited to receive a new life into our family. What will it be? How will we manage? Many groans and complaints have gone up to God. "O God, we ask you for a healthy child!"

Before this knot of waiting was untied, a second knot came into the rope of our lives, a new teaching position. This, what should have happened two years ago, has happened now. The school at Alexandrowka has dismissed me. So, away from Siberia! Now to our home! Our hearts were filled with joy to see our parents and relatives again, but at the same time, we had an overwhelming concern: where will we spend the winter? We had not received any news from our parents about a place for us there. Too much was happening at one time in our life.

It happened on June 29. I would not say that Suse was exactly uncomfortable during the day, but something special was in the air. The usual labor pains began in the evening and the midwife came at about 6 o'clock. From 8 o'clock on it became intense. The clock showed that time went by, but it seemed to us that the all seemed to stand still. The Lord helped and finally on June 30 at 1:20 in the morning a son was born to me, Harry.

What a big step my son has taken from the mysterious kingdom of not being to a sorrowful world on an accursed earth! Soon thereafter Suse felt quite comfortable. The Lord has given great things to us! Lord, I pray, consecrate this small one to yourself and open our eyes to understanding in order to raise him in your way!

On Tuesday, August 1, three carriages came for us and we left happily toward our new home. After we had driven awhile from Alexandrowka, the clouds parted and the sun won over the sky. On Wednesday, I returned to get the last things and now nothing tied us to pretty Alexandrowka.

For four years we had experienced both joy and sorrow in Alexandrowka. We prayed. God, you alone can make our move into our new home a blessing to us and to others! Please give to our earnest intentions also the fulfillment!

Amen!

Thanksgiving Services

After settling into their new home, (an extremely stressful activity for the family) Wieler attended Thanksgiving services in several towns. Here, in his journals, he begins to record the sermons by paraphrasing them after the event.

During the autumn months, Wieler resumed his practice of photography as a means of supplemental income

Thanksgiving Service in Margenau.

Thanksgiving service in Margenau was held on October 15, and I had the pleasure of attending. In the morning, a friend preached about the fire where Peter had warmed himself—a strange fire! In the afternoon, there was a wedding. Heinrich Franz Neufeld married Mr. Janzen's daughter Marie. After the ceremony, the bride and groom came to us and allowed themselves to be photographed for portraits.

Thanksgiving Service in Halbstadt.

The Thanksgiving service in Halbstadt was scheduled for October 22, and I really wanted to go there as well. Many people left on Saturday morning, I could not and I really did not want to go alone. Our friend, Giesbrecht went with his daughter and her friend on Saturday night so I went along with them. We arrived there at 4 o'clock in the morning. Now where should we go at this hour of the day? Into the chapel! It was extremely cold and we lay down for a while to rest. After a morning breakfast, the rooms in the chapel soon filled with people from far and near.

One song after another resounded upwards through the chapel. Happy, "Zion's Songs," pulled our hearts upward to God, who has prepared Zion for us. "Sounds of Home" moved our souls that they cried triumphantly about the "good news" of our imminent return home. Our loud "Believer's voice" rose to praise the Redeemer and Savior. That is how it happened that before the worship service even began one had already been blessed. The wise Brother Krüger gave the invocation with the hymn Neq 548, 1-3. Then he read Psalm. 104, 24.27.34 (Miniaturb.33.)

The Psalmist saw God's great creation! The order in God's creation moved him. Lord, your creation is great!

Brother Krüger spoke:

In spring we were so worried, the dry storms had destroyed many of our seeds. At that point, we expected that of which Jeremiah spoke about. Summer is passed and we have not received any help! In addition, how do we fare now? See how unending the works of God are! He has given us such rich blessings!

A brother told me how he and many others had gone into the fields in the spring to cry to the Lord! Your crying was not in vain. The Lord gives when he knows it is time! When the drought was greatest his help was at its nearest.

Many prayers went up from the people, most said, "Lord, I can not thank you as much as you have done for me!"

Then Brother Krüger welcomed the guests and spoke about a twofold sacrifice: Prayer and Money. Later, preacher Jonathan Braun, who also had been a refugee from Volhynia, spoke to the congregation. He began with the hymn Neq 241,1 from Glbst.

In his introductory remarks, he stated that he was taking care of his father-in-law who was ill, and whom he had left for only a short time. He had hurried here in order to enjoy the fellowship. Without prior knowledge, he happened upon a thanksgiving service and was asked to preach there. He however declined because he was not prepared for it. Then, a second person was asked, then a third, etc. Everyone gave the same answer. Then he jumped up and said, ?I thank God that I am allowed to preach!" Since he did not know anything about the Thanksgiving service, he could not preach a righteous Thanksgiving sermon, but he would preach what he had in hand. He read from Hebrews 2:17,18 and Luke 4:1-4.

The temptation of Jesus is divided into 4 parts:
1. Temptation during the 40 days.
2. The first attack.
3. The second attack
4. The third attack.

We define temptation as to be tempted to do something evil. Only true believers are tempted to do something evil. A master had a coachman; the coachman was a believer and the master was not. Many times the coachman complained about temptation. To the complaints the master just laughed, he did not have any temptations! The coachman could not explain why this was so. One day they went hunting together; the master hunted ducks. One of the ducks fell dead into a culvert, whereas another was simply wounded and flew on. The master ignored the first one as he chased after the second one.

It then became clear to the coachman, "master, now I know why you do not have any temptations! You are a dead duck!"

He has the unbelievers for his advantage. For what was Christ tempted with? He was tempted with everything. Hebrews 2.

1. Temptation during the 40 days! After the baptism, there was temptation and for us it is no different. Our temptation began after our baptism. We see the failings of others, and through much more we are tempted.

Jesus was the first filled with the Holy Spirit! How loving of God! Jesus was filled with the Holy Spirit after being certain that God was well pleased with Him, His beloved Son. After this certainty came a solid foundation, and thus the lure into the temptation. It is no different for us!

Jesus was led by the Spirit! Was not the evil one filled with the Holy Spirit? No, it was not the same Spirit who had filled him! It is told to us that God does not tempt anyone! Still, God tempted Abraham.

Why does God tempt? God tempts us in order to deny the devil a reason for blasphemy. Satan could have said, "Yes, yes! Your beloved Son; you have him in your possession! One can not harm him! No wonder he remains without sin!"

Jesus should be like his brother and feel with him. Now he knows how we are tormented by the devil: in those forty days he lived through everything! How the devil tempted him during that time is not stated. The one thing we know is that he was tempted just like us!

Where was Jesus tempted? In the desert! And, why there exactly? It was a test of his faith. We are all faithful when we can be seen by our fellow man. However, if we are not always observed, then we are not so careful to be without sin. In the desert the temptation was much greater for Jesus for no one saw him there! None but the Lord! What man would have known what he did there? Jesus was always aware of his position!

Temptation has limits. Twice God set limits, particular limits, for Satan concerning Job. Note the significance of forty days. Moses, he who received the law on the mountain, had forty days. Jesus, the person who fulfilled the law, was tempted for 40 days.

2. The forty days are full. The devil oversteps the limit and ponders a dark attack; he ponders the biggest attack of all. Satan does not shrink away from the Son of God! He will then come at us! How much more will he be willing to tempt us! Satan knows who Jesus is and knows his works! We can learn from him.

Do you know that feeling in the pit of your stomach? That is Satan seizing an opportunity. We should learn! Jesus yearns for us and He adapts to the opportunities before Him. He offers bread, not gold! By us he does the same. He takes the side from which we say: that is my nature, my temperament!

The Lord has blessed the harvest here richly. It is my wish that there will be a rich harvest of the Spirit this winter! Amen.

Brother Regiehr, of Margenau, spoke next and encouraged us, "that in regard to all we have heard, we must hold on to what we have!" He read Matthew 26:69-75 and Hymns Neq 3/5, 1-3 (Glbst.).

If we say that we are not concerned with denial now because everything is full we are misguided! That is not true trust in God! True trust in God shows itself when everything is empty.

O pray, that we uphold God's Word! Dark times are coming! Psalm 146.

How did it happen that Peter denied the Lord? It was the fact that he was not near Jesus! His pride was the first step away from Jesus. His sleep in the garden was the second step. Today, we also sleep! He struck when he should have shown love (Malchus). That is the third step! He warmed himself by a strange fire—the fourth step! Do you stay warm by a strange fire? The time will come when we will be tested, hold close to His Word, He protects so willingly! Peter's fall was great, how long will we fall? Peter had preference before others for he was there, beside Jesus, where others were not allowed. He was warned. And were we warned? Our fall will be greater for we were warned often!

But, Peter did not remain still and away. He came back to Jesus. How did he come back to the Lord? His first step was that he remembered what Jesus had said, and Jesus was correct. Jesus' loving glance was the second step. Then Peter approached Him—the third step. O, we should approach Him now, not later when we must approach Him!

A certain servant wanted to strike his master. Later he approached his master in the hospital, where he was. The latter only asked this, "Why did you strike me?"

Such a confrontation! And, when you are before Jesus, will Jesus ask you: Why did you strike me?

Benediction with Hymn 38,1-4. The sermon was followed by a noon break.

During the noon break, the same thing happened as in the morning. The rooms gradually filled with people returning for the word of God and one song after another rang upwards.

After the break, the first speaker was Brother Haman. He began with the hymn Neq 224, 1-2 and read Lk.12:13-21. The mission sermon followed and was delivered by Brother Dücks. Zion l. Neq 147, 1-3. Joh.4:27ff (-39). Verse 34.

Jesus' mission: He knew exactly what His mission was. Jesus did not let any opportunity or resource remain unused, and this is also our task. He could not live without doing missions. His mission is the harvest!

1. Mission field. White unto harvest. Lift up your eyes. The kingdom of God is ripe unto harvest. Up! Away from us! The field is ready! Lift up your eyes!

2. Mission task. Take up the work. We have three tasks: spread the seed, intercession, and sacrifice. We must sacrifice our gifts, our earthly possessions! We must pay our debts. He who does not pay his earthly debts is bankrupt and is a deceiver.

3. Mission blessing. Wage! We gain the fruit for all eternity.

Psalm 126:5. Hymn Neq 400 Glbst.

This was followed by another Benediction and time for coffee. There was scheduled another service in the evening, but those of us who had traveled from a great distance began our journey home after coffee. Quite a large group gathered in the second class waiting hall at Moskalenki station. At the station we waited until one o'clock in the morning for a train. The time was well spent as the son of one of the speakers entertained us.

At two o'clock we arrived at the station. Some men went to secure carriages for our drive. At four o'clock I arrived at home.

(Later I found out that there was a Thanksgiving service in Alexandrowka on October 29.)

Braun's Sermon

In November, the town had an exciting visitor by the name of D. Braun. It is evident through Wieler's praise that Braun was a member of the church who was greatly respected and personally liked by all of the community. Wieler records the events of that visit.

5 November 5, 1917
Sunday, 6:30 in the morning
Yesterday evening we received the unexpected news that a preacher would visit us and that there was to be an evening service. Preacher D. Braun had arrived from Waldheim.

I want to write down a few things about his sermon. It depends on you, you great God, my father, if I am up to this task or not. It depends on you if this entry can be a blessing, for me and later for my kin. But, no, not only on you, I must allow your Spirit to guide me; He will empty me of the evening's events and in turn fill me from on high. We know, from you, that you are prepared to bless! So Lord, let me be a conduit through which your blessing can stream down, first to our family, then to the closest region and then on to the entire world beyond! Until then you have not won authority over me. Forgive!

Genesis 6:3-12

Here and there the question is asked, "How will it be when Jesus comes?"

Now and then one notices that the time is near and one asks, "How will it be?"

Jesus said at one time: It will be as in the time of Noah; they ate, drank, courted and allowed themselves to be courted. So, it will also be in the days of the Son of Man as it was in the time of Noah. How was it then?

Verse 3. People do not want to allow my Spirit to punish them! And today, what do we allow? I could say much about the unbelievers who do not even respond to the Spirit's exhortation. I could say much about believers; woe to him if the Spirit has to stir him with hammer blows of his conscience! God did not give man a conscience just so that he would have one. It is also true that today men do not allow the Spirit to punish them.

Verse 4. Tyrants! They are mighty! It is wonderful that among unbelievers there are so many huge men. That is how it is today also! There are men who can captivate thousands of people with their speeches. I thank God that we have singers who have gifts which they use for the glory of God. A person can inspire thousands through singing, all that only for the entertainment of people. Amazing! God freely offers his gifts. In every person he plants a seed and then watches how it unfolds.

Verse 5. The imagination of the thoughts of the heart was evil. What does the imagination of the heart mean? Well, imagination remains imagination and thoughts remain thoughts. The Bible means what it says. When we today have poets and composers, instrumentalists, etc. whose nice songs we sing, it gives also thousands of honorable men who spend their lives composing and writing and everything just to completely expose humanity's complete loathing of sin. Go into the book stores of the big city! Will you find informative books? You will find only filth! You will find sin complete and exposed! The imagination of the thoughts of the heart are evil, today as it was in Noah's time!

One thing in that teaching does not agree with today's time! It says, "the earth is corrupted!"

Yes, then it probably was, but it is not today!

If I had the intellectuals of today before me this evening and I would say the earth is corrupt, one would look at me pitifully and commiserate with me from the heart. Then the man of knowledge would stand up and say, "Young man! See how far knowledge has advanced. You say the earth is corrupt? Come with me and see the achievements of knowledge. We have made excavations that tell the history of antiquity. We see the past as if it were today! We have found trees that we can tell have been standing for 6,000 years. We are so advanced in our knowledge that for every one of your questions we can give you a knowledge based and thoroughly thought through answer. Then you say the earth is corrupt! No!"

The man of modern research would stand up and say, "The earth corrupt? Well, you are just young. Now say, what has been discovered which has improved the earth? What would one do without petroleum, without naphtha, without electricity? What would one do without all the discoveries of recent times? Yes, before, when man had to plough his fields with a wooden plough, when he had to seed his corn by hand, when he had to cut his grain by hand with the sickle and thrash it by flail, when he had to make his flour for bread with a hand-mill, then I would respect your statement. I do not agree with you now, not today when we have a machine for every task and human power has become unnecessary! People do not have to go on foot today. People travel by railway, by electric means, in steamships and submarines; they fly in the air. Man has subjugated everything. In the big cities, they live as if they were in a small paradise! Is the earth corrupt? No!"

In the same way many would present the good things of this earth and thereby show that the earth is not corrupt! In spite of all that I maintain to you: The earth is corrupt!

The 18 million people who are being murdered today cry to heaven, "the earth is corrupt!"

Man's blood, which soaks every small part of our earth, cries to the Creator, "the earth is corrupt!"

The clothes we wear on our bodies, every thread of the same cries to us, "The earth is corrupt! Corrupt!"

Every piece of bread, which we put in our mouths, sighs, "Corrupt! Corrupt!"

On every crumb of the same hangs swindle and deceit without end! People, the earth is corrupt, in spite of everything that people do to make it seem beautiful! The earth is corrupt. That is the position today to their God! In opposition, let us look at God's position! He has patience! For 120 years he waited!

Then he had regret! He regretted that he had created man.

The Lord had regret?

Yes, regret!

You ask, "Then the Bible is contradicting itself. It does say in one place that God is not a human, so that he does not regret anything!"

No, God's Word can not contradict itself! It happens like it did to the child.... Before the child was a table with money on it. There is gold, silver, copper and paper money on the table. We tell the child, "that is money!"

We show a copper coin: that is copper money. Further, we say to him: that is silver money and that is paper money! When we ask about each single piece he will answer correctly; that that is copper money, or that is silver money! That is paper money! If we take a gold piece and ask the child, "what is this?"

Money! It has not been explained to the child, it is just money! That is how we experience God's regret! He gives various regrets, we however have just one word for regret; more words have not been given to us.

And now you, dear listener, God has patience but that patience does have an end. The 120 years also had an end. You say with Nineveh he had forty days of patience, with Israel forty years, etc., with me he will have patience at least until tomorrow! Yes, but who will guarantee that the forty days are not already over tonight. And what will happen to us then?

That is what Braun said! He could present it so well and make it so clear. I cannot record it from memory exactly, but this gives the content of his sermon.

Two Sermons

ere, Wieler took the time to record into his journals a two part Sunday sermon. One part of the sermon was given by Brother Wall who resided in a neighboring community, and another by the aforementioned Brother Braun.

November 9, 1917
We have now traded the wheels on our wagons for blades on our winter sleds. In spite of that fact the weather is quite good! We are beginning to talk about the Christmas Eve program. Many special preparations and dedicated hours go into this event.

I now want to enter some things about the Sunday sermons of Braun. This is my first impression of the morning. Brother Wall made the invocation after the prayer hour.

Two men stood by a stream. The one man knew the source of it and the other did not. The man who did not know the source saw the stream as it was before him and said, "This stream will soon dry up!"

"Oh no!" replied the other. "I know the source of this stream and it will never dry up!"

The Bible is like that stream, and its source is Jesus, it can never dry up. Streams flow into the sea, and the stream of the Bible flows into God. Lk.19:10.

When I leave on a journey I always take my staff with me. Without my staff, I do not go out. I am always happy when I have my staff and it seems to fit so well in my hand. No other staff could fit so well. God's Word is like a staff to me, I am supported so well by it. Yes, someone will say, this man takes the most familiar verse out of the whole Bible. Exactly! That is what I wanted. It just fits into my hand. For me it is as if it was always new.

The brothers were pleased that I was willing to travel with them on this slippery road. They knew what they wanted and would have here today through my sermon. That is good. They knew their own purpose just as Jesus knew why he had come: to seek. Before the foundation of the world, God held a consultation.

Who can redeem humanity? Probably a cherub came and covered his face with his wings and said, "I can not do that!"

Then comes one and with a lovely voice says, "Father, I will do it!"

"Yes, my son, you are capable of doing it!" And, when the time was fulfilled, God sent his Son. Jesus knew why.

There are various seekers in the world. Many understand how to seek and others do not. This is an experience we find in our children. I ask at breakfast, "Children, tell me a suitable hymn for this or that text!"

"But father! Take this and this number as your answer!"

And I am saved! I look thoroughly! "Where are my galoshes?"

One child finds them and brings them to me. The others looked through the entire house for them. Yes, there are various seekers in our world, but Jesus is the best seeker. We can measure ourselves against him. We must think about our fellow human being.

We will soon be at the end of our existence. Then, we must rely on Jesus. There we hardly have to wash because Jesus seeks! Yet, people are full of wickedness. Jesus was seeking their souls and they asked him if it was right to heal of the Sabbath? It bounces off and is ignored. Did he find anyone? Oh yes!

He sought Saul before the gates of Damascus and found Paul. "I count all things but dung, that I may win Christ!" (see Philippians 3:8)

There is a man named Jairus. "But Jairus, why are you going to Jesus?"

"Well, my child is deathly ill!" Jesus seeks, and as he is going to Jairus something else happens. A woman, crooked from years of illness, presses through the crowd until she reaches Him. She just wants to touch him. She does it. She wants to leave again. . . . Wait! "Who touched me?"

Listen to the rational disciples and what they say, "In that crowd someone is always touching you!"

"Some power has left me!"

Jesus found many.

And so on!

Brother Braun:

Matthew 3:1-12.

If a king wants to explain a war or wants to visit, he will send a harbinger first! John was such a harbinger of the king Jesus, to explain the war to his archenemy Satan. The harbinger's message contains the following:

    1. The demands of the kingdom.
    2. Warning of the appointment by preference.
    3. The seriousness of the era.

1. If one emigrates to another kingdom, one first studies the laws of the land because he will have to obey them as well as claim his rights in his new homeland. So also must man do here.

Penance! Penance from atonement. So, are we to torment ourselves, chastise ourselves, fast, put our feet into shoes with nails sticking out and walk long distances, slide up and down the steps of St. Peters Basilica in Rome—in short, are we to make atonement? No.

Penance means repentance, to change one's attitude or conversion. It means that which one person stated, "Burn what you have prayed to! Pray to what you have burned!"

Confess your sins! Yes, we are missing that today. Where do we have the custom today where a priest allows sins to be confessed to him? Where is the time of the auricular confession? Where are the break chairs and the benches on which the sinner kneels and in which the priest puts his ear to the small opening and hears an accounting of your sins? When the Jews descended to be baptized, they gave up their self-righteousness. Everything of man's own fell away.

Baptism! John's baptism was not the baptism of Romans 6:3-4. Acts 19:1 ff.

Produce worthy fruit! In this world there are many unworthy fruits. Worthy fruits are peace and joy in your heart, peace with all people. Do not unbelievers also produce such fruit? Yes, those are wild fruits, not produced out of love for God!

2. John warned us to not appoint ourselves by precedence. The Jews did it, and here is the precedence:

Abraham. We have Abraham as our father as we are descended from him. He had the promise that all his descendants on earth would be blessed. Would the children of such a man ever be lost? Never! Yet, it is different today.

"What, I will not be saved? Yes. You have not known my parents! Oh, they were very pious people! Oh, my mother, she prayed! And I, a child of such parents, am lost? God can not do that!"

And yet you will be lost! You can not be born into your spiritual nobleness. You can only be born into human nobleness!

Israel. We belong to Israel, God's chosen people! Is that not guarantee enough? We are the bearers of promise! Listen to the people say that we should convert!

"What," replies the man, "How can I be lost? I belong to an only saving church! I am a Lutheran, Baptist, and belong to this and that church, to the council of full communion etc. etc. You should have read what our forefathers suffered because of their faith! The blood of our martyrs will open the gates of heaven for us!"

I say to you, "if you were 10,000 times a Baptist, if you were baptized 10,000 times, in spite of all that, you are lost, irredeemably lost!"

Ceremony. The Jews had sacrifices, prescribed cleansing, they had order for their feasts and their prayer times, and depended on them. And what do we do? I do everything: attend services, communion, I am baptized, I am a Sunday School teacher, I sing and pray, and have prayer meetings. Nevertheless, if your heart is not in it, then you will be judged accordingly.

The Pharisees are the leaders of the religious council, and depended on by us. John however warned them to show their fruits. We also have not reason to hope. Or, it will be for us like it was for Samson's jawbone of a donkey; Samson used it, as long as he wanted, and then he threw it away.

3. The time is serious. The axe is already at the roots of the tree and Israel is the tree. God has spared the Jews, the natural branch! Will he spare us, the wild ones? The axe is at your life's tree. He is waiting! Maybe there will be some buds! He will baptize with fire and fire consumes everything that is impure! He has the winnowing-shovel in his hand. Chaff and wheat are mixed together and only God sees the heart. He throws the chaff and wheat into the wind, into the wind of tribulation, of temptation!

Today a storm is approaching; the storm of God's wrath. One can hear this. The chaff and wheat will ultimately separate!

The Coming of the Holidays

Wieler was often in charge of producing the Christmas program for the community. This was a responsibility that he cherished greatly. Although the extra work often conflicted with his own personal and professional endeavors, he believed the works of the church, great or small, should come first in a person's life. This is only one way in which the church could take precedence over his own life.

November 15, 1917
    Wednesday.
    We had a nice autumn day today! Spring foreboding went through my mind, I dreamt of wonderful weather where the snow had completely disappeared.
    We began our preparations for the evangelistic evening today. I had some of the youth here and I read to them about the rotten son "David."
    We are also busy with the Christmas Eve preparations. It is coming closer all the time.
Lilly was very ill at home, but is now on the road to recovery!

November 23, 1917
    In the evening.
    From the schoolroom, sound echoes across to us: rehearsal time! The singers are practicing familiar songs. Also in preparation is an evangelistic evening that is to be held December 3. This was just decided yesterday.

We decided not to do "David" for the Christmas Eve program but instead chose "Naaman." I have assigned all the characters and the process of learning lines has begun. Everything that will be accomplished depends on you, almighty God and Father. From the bottom of my heart I ask you, you omnipresent One, be our helper in preparation and our leader on that evening! We ask that there be streams of blessing, nothing less! You have promised it, Father! Remember your Word! Protect me, oh Holy Spirit, from Satan, who puts in my path the demons of conceit and egotism! Lord, take over the whole thing! It is yours!

Amen!

November 24, 1917

We just had guests! The Epp family was here. They came for a short hour and brought us school books, Bible stories and short readers. The primers I have ordered for class have still not arrived! The people are getting impatient, and I am not really at fault! In such situations, one would like to hang up on the nail the schoolmaster's mantel if it was possible!

From you, oh Father in heaven, I now ask: make it so that the package with primers will soon arrive! Your arm is not too short to give the postal service a shove. The package was posted on September 14. Lord, in spite of everything going at a snail's pace nowadays, I expect, from you, the imminent arrival of the primers! By your Word's will!

Amen!

December 7, 1917

We are very busy with preparations for Christmas Eve. The youth are helping.

December 19, 1917)

One day follows another. Life flows by so calmly and proportionately quietly!

We only know and see what is happening in our immediate area. Far away from us things could be occurring which could deeply affect us and affect the lives of our dearest on earth! What is man?

Today we received news that my father is very ill. From November 6 on, he has been ill and since December 5, he is in Halbstadt to help him regain his strength. And where is he today? Who knows? Maybe he is already long since resting in the cool earth! For him it would be victory, but for her, my mother... Lord, be near to her! If it is not against your plans, keep him for her! If not, please comfort her! Give us, the children, correct wisdom, to be for her what we ought to be!

Now I do not know what to do, should I go there to him or wait here? Maybe we will receive news!

December 23, 1917)

Saturday! The day after tomorrow the holidays begin! The day before yesterday was my father's 59th birthday. I wonder if he has experienced it? Who knows how it is? O Father in Heaven, alleviate his pain! If you take him home, please support my mother!

December 25, 1917

Christmas!

The first day of holidays is behind us. Time flies! How well did the parents experience this day? Is Father still alive? If only news would come again!

Yesterday evening took it right out of me! At night, I had no rest. In confusing dream pictures the happenings of yesterday evening fluttered by me. Spiritually, I was more tired when I arose from my sleep, bodily I probably rested. When I came home yesterday evening, I could hardly stay upright. The evening lasted 3 and a half hours, and before that, I was already on my feet since noon.

I threw myself on the bed and listened, if one could hear, to the pain that raged through every limb! Then I had a very disagreeable thought; yes, you have overexerted yourself this time and are nearly ill and no one cares about you. No one has a word of thanks or acknowledgement for you! I closed my eyes and did not want to have any more thoughts. The door

opened and someone came in. My top student was here and brought with him a letter. I opened it and read:
On behalf of the village, permit me to convey to you our heartfelt thanks for your work. Enclosed is a small gift.
    50 Rubles were enclosed!
    While I was writing a short reply someone else came. She brought an envelope from old Brother M. Krüger. He also wrote about acknowledgement and praise, so that I rather not record the letter here because I did not earn such praise! I was less happy because it implicated me in the future to strive more for the better performance of my duty.
    25 Rubles were enclosed!
    After the end of the Christmas Eve program I had received 15 Rubles from Mrs. Bäcker while still in the chapel. I am overwhelmed by all the chickens, ducks, and doves which were brought to us. In short, we felt loved, which felt very good! It is very difficult for us as humans to work without reaping some reward! That is a sign of false attitude!

December 30, 1917
    The journey is behind me! I came home at noon today, yet home was not home because Suse was not here. When I left in the afternoon, I went into the village because a new village mayor was being elected.
    Suse was still not home when I returned. She probably will not come today.
    Today we have thawing weather. I think of how my father may be doing! No news!
    Suse has returned.

New Year's Eve! With our friends, the Kraus's, we could pour out our hearts before the Lord. Blessed minutes! More than if it had been hours!

We were already asleep when we were awakened suddenly by singing. Suse and I looked at each other: What was that? Where is it coming from?

We noticed the singing was coming from outside our window. This act of love was done for us and many others by August and Wilhelm Risto and the daughters of our friends, the Krause's. It was a wonderful surprise.

1918

Winter 1918

Prayers for Health, Friendship and Deliverance

During the winter of 1918, Wieler learns that he may not be living in a place where he would like to remain. He feels pressure from community members who question his effectiveness as a teacher. On January 31 he writes that he overheard a townsperson say, "The teacher is careful. He thinks that if he gives us his little finger we will take his whole hand." Wieler seems to take this as an insult, and believes that people are mistrusting of him.

Suse continues her work as a midwife.

After some consideration, Henry and Suse begin preparations to leave Siberia. During this time the Russian calendar changes.

January 31, 1918

It appears that we will not escape the turmoil of winter this year. My wife, Suse, is always tediously working on one thing or another. She takes care of the children. She takes care of her patients, often calling upon them in their homes. We often have guests that she must prepare for. There is sewing, washing, mending, darning, and various other things that come up for her to do.

Besides all that work, she is not well. The influenza, which has invaded so many homes, appears to have entered ours. This foul sickness has entered her body and gives her little rest. Also, her teeth hurt; they give her pain during every meal whenever she tries to eat the littlest thing.

Yesterday we had the Heinrichs over as guests. We brought to close our monetary matters with him, soon we will not owe anyone in Siberia anything. It is a great feeling!

God is blessing our work! He is a patient God! We owe the Lord so much for the years 1916 and 1917. We have prayed to Him. "First pay off our debts," we asked. "Then, Lord, we want to pay you our solemn promise!"

See us Lord! The debts are being paid off. If God preserves us from harm we will have our debts all paid by May. O Creator of the Earth and great Father of your poor children, we want to fulfill our promise. It all depends on your almighty hand! Help us as you have so wonderfully helped us until now. A year ago our debts were in the thousands, and in this year we hope to pay them all off.

Ebenezer! Lord, take our affairs into your hands from now on, for then it will be always good for us! Amen!

February 4, 1918

A wonderful and clear Sunday, the sky is without clouds. In the afternoon we had unexpected guests. Heinrich Reimer, having recently returned from Crimea, visited with his two sisters. During his trip he visited the Alexandertal Colony, and brought a letter from our friend Jonathan Sukkau. The letter included a photo of Jonathan and his wife. Old real estate matters had given the correspondence between Jonathan and I a critical tone, so much that I thought our friendship had ended. This letter proves my thinking was misguided. We can shake hands with brotherly love and friendship despite a disagreement over land trade.

Thanks be to God! He has given me a friend truly worthy of the name Jonathan. A friend whose trustworthiness comes closer to God's than many men, including myself. Lord, reward him with an inexhaustible spiritual power from You!

February 21, 1918

This afternoon the new village authorities discussed the town's condition and order. This discussion yielded no conclusion. Good! God will make it so that any matter will be resolved in a way that benefits his servants!

February 24, 1918

Mr. Steinborm preached our Sermon today. He held a rather interesting sermon concerning the words of John: Children, it is the last hour!

What will end in the last hour?

For many years, Germany and Russia have lived in peace. Now, the last hour of this peaceful relationship has come. We had predicted that the German ambassador would be recalled. His work in Russia has ended. In this same way will the ambassador of God be recalled when his work on Earth has ended.

When war was declared we received no news from abroad. In Russia, no more information was given to us about Kaiser William. It is the proclamation of the Gospel, in the same way will God allow our last hour to arrive.

What will begin when the last hour arrives?

There will come a judgment of the godless unbelievers, and those who have fallen away from the word of God.

There will come a time of comfort for the believers.

In the evening we listened to Adam Georg preach the love of the Father. For God so loved the world that he gave his only begotten Son, that whoever believes in him shall not perish but shall have everlasting life.

February 28, 1918

According to the calendar, today is the last day of February. It has been a short month and we have been given good weather. What January has given us in snowstorms, February has amended with bright sunshine and clear weather.

I have had delivered a pair of shoes to the house for me. For these new shoes, I am to pay 100 rubles. Since the forming of our new government, prices have dramatically increased.

Yesterday and today we have not been well. The little ones, Lilly and Harry, have been coughing. Suse and I have an illness that is affecting our head and throat. We fear it may be the whooping cough which is ravaging quite a few homes here. If you, O God, do not protect us, then we will soon be there with you. You can protect us. Do whatever your holy will finds good for us! Amen.

March 2, 1918 (morning)
All this morning the village was full of sleighs as more guests arrived for the conference. I am anxious to know what will happen today; I have never experienced anything like this before. The conference is supposed to begin today at 8 o'clock. It is now seven.

Last evening we held the introduction for the conference taking place today.

Having time before the meeting starts, I'd like to put down the contents of the invocation made yesterday as I had taken notes.

A festive mood hung over the gathered delegates when I entered the chapel. At the beginning the choir sang five songs: Our Journey, In the Closet, Rescue Whom You Can, Never Alone and Just as I am. After the singing, Brother Schröder from Turgai gave the invocation. The text which was read was 1 Joh.1:3-7.

Why does John direct such words at believers? The love of Jesus forces him to do it! He speaks of the love the Father has shown for us, especially for me! I was in darkness, had fellowship with darkness and hated the light. Jesus redeemed me.

Now I have fellowship with God, the Father, with his Son, with the Light! What a fellowship! What we have seen and heard, what we have experienced, we declare to You! One may have had fellowship with darkness, now he has fellowship with God! But before fellowship with God one must put off darkness. We must become clean!

How is this reflected in life? If one wants to preserve something in a container, one examines the container and cleans the inside. If one does not follow these steps the clean thing which is put into the container will become dirty, ill preserved fruit will spoil.

The darkness, the sin, has to be cleaned out. Many now think that nothing will separate them from fellowship with God! Beware, do not relax!

When we have fellowship with God, then we also have fellowship with one another; John writes this so that your joy may be complete! Tell it to others, so that they can rejoice with you! If a child receives a gift, that child will go from one person to another telling their good fortune. We rejoice with that child. Tell the Word to others, then your joy will become great; it will be complete. Only then will you have fellowship with Jesus.

His blood cleanses us from all sin! We are clean!

Although, we can not say that we are still without sin. We still need cleansing, we need other fellowship... fellowship with Jesus and fellowship with one another. The fellowship between men makes us happy and content in life; it makes our joy great and makes us complete!

We experience many things when we have fellowship with one another. Fellowship can not be neglected if we are to be children of Light! Joy is then in us. We have joy in Him. And after this joy we have the blessed hope, the hope to be with Him who has redeemed us! To see Him as He is! O complete joy! Rejoice in the Lord! And again I say to you: rejoice! Amen.

Then, the second speaker, Brother Schmidtfall, stood up. Meaning well, with all the feeling and heart he could muster, he tried to address the congregation. He worked with full voice to be heard in the entire chapel room, but with all his energy he could not manage it. Everything about him reflected sympathy. His prayer was not written out, and still one had the impression that everything was very logical.

Your work, Lord, you have not entrusted to angels or seraphim, but to incapable people! He spoke from the Gospel of Matthew 9:37 & 38.

What is the occasion for the words of Mathew: Jesus was making his way with some disciples through various marketplaces. His penetrating eyes saw the hearts of men and he could see that they desire happiness. But, he did not see this in the actions or treatment of the people. He saw the misery of mankind, their restlessness, their dissention! This grieved him! What a heart! What sympathy! His heart is full of compassion, and in that context he speaks those words.

Today, He also looks at mankind. It grieves him! He sees the divine harvest field and speaks about the extent of it, the need and what we have to do about it.

The harvest field of the Lord is great, it is the entire universe! No person from the entire universe is excluded and the colour of the skin makes no difference. No one is excluded. Whether the white European or the red Indian, or the black Negro or the yellow Japanese and Chinese, or even I—we are all God's harvest field! The work is plentiful! All people are bought with blood. That is why the enemy is in such a rage. We are confident, sealed with the Holy Spirit; that is our eternal right.

The harvest field is big and—ripe! There are but few workers! When Jesus spoke these words there were twelve men listening. They were, however, prepared in the master's seminar, with His own words. Jesus also saw that one of these few would not work the harvest field. On this one man the effort and education is lost! His name was Judas. Later, the Lord sends out 70 disciples, more workers. The work of the Lord does not stand still. Today there are more workers than in the days of the bible, but the truth still holds: there are not enough reapers! There is much to do today. The end is near! There is little time in prospect! Besides that there is freedom! Take advantage and use this free time.

It appears today that the workers in the world have fallen asleep! They race about, chasing after treasures, accumulating that wretched paper money! We are much better Christians if we are put in, beat and not allowed such work. Not so long ago when we were still in a soldier's uniform and we were forbidden to use our mother tongue and read God's Word, we went into the forest to pray. That is blessed fellowship!

The Lord Jesus gives us the duty. . . . pray to the Lord of the harvest, that He will send forth labourers into His harvest! The Lord of the harvest in God, the Father!

Were not the angels prepared to work? We have the right to ask Him! On wings from the heavens, why are there no

angels descending to work the fields of the Lord? Would they not have gladly gone into the harvest field to serve Him?
Yes!

In spite of that desire, it is not the angels, but the people whom He has given His work! Pray the Lord of the harvest!

This demand is not difficult, this request is not a difficult task that He sends! He calls the workers! He sends them! All his epistles which the apostle Paul wrote include a divine calling. Paul did not come on his own accord, the Lord called him!

God prepares his workers with diligence, so that they may work their entire lives until their final evening comes! Today, some workers sigh so much and complain, but diligent workers, sent by God, do not know anything about sighing and complaining. God has prepared them with power!

When He gives assignments, He also gives the power to carry them out, so that His workers do not know anything about getting tired. The Lord of the harvest fills His workers with the love of Christ, with this preparation they can do nothing but work untiringly. The love of Christ compels us.

There will also be results!

He gives his workers the Holy Spirit because they have studied God's Word. This prepared worker now has the necessary light for the work—light for life's way, light concerning the Word, light concerning oneself! If the light is missing, the workers are incapable of work! This Spirit, the Holy Spirit, only lives in clean hearts!

Those workers, which He has sent into the harvest, know exactly how and where they are to begin their work. They do not have to take time to ask, "what is my work?" They know what their work is!

Where are the workers? Who are they?

1. The preachers. Big duties and particular responsibilities lie on us. Cursed is he who is negligent in doing the work of the Lord! They are not to despair, He, after all, prepares them! That the work appears so difficult and weighs so heavily on them only comes in hindsight to them. Look to

Him who has sent you and, in whose service, your work is secure!

2. The Deacons. They are also called to service. The word 'deacon' means servant. Their duties are great and nice and necessary!

3. The Sunday School Teacher. They have been assigned work that is indispensable. It is the most blessed work!

4. The Singers. Sing! Sing! Even if the enemy tries by every means to make your work ineffective! Sing! Even if a chill wind should blow on you and take away your desire. Sing! Sing!

No one is free! Work is always there! The wheat is ripe, it is ready to cut, and so everyone must go to work! Each one must testify! Everyone!

Sister, the work for you is not trifling! You must lead the children to Jesus. You are the ones who plant the first seeds in their small, open hearts when you teach them to fold their hands and pray their first prayer!

Pray to the Lord of the harvest! If the disciples had not responded to the call of the Lord and instead stayed at the tax collector's table, or stayed seated by their fishing nets, we would not have the gospel today! Ask and be willing to work! Are we working in order to have sheaves!

There must be means to work! When the farmer sees that the wheat is ripe he sees to it that he has the money to harvest it! God has given money! There will be many who moan while departing with their money, "I give and always give!" God loves the cheerful giver! Give and you will have more to give. The Lord himself says, "bring me all your tithes and prove me, if I will not open the windows of heaven!" Give to the Lord, our blessed privilege! May the Lord give us a heart like His! May we grieve for the nations! Amen!

The Siberian Baptists

In the winter of 1918, German Christian leaders from ten different areas of Siberia descended upon Wieler's small town of Alexandrowka. The purpose of the conference was to establish a working bond between the German Christian communities in the Siberian region. What follows are notes taken by Wieler during the meeting.

The name used in the original translation, the First General Federated Conference of West Siberia (i.e. Siberian Baptists), is probably a loose, inaccurate translation. Translators agree that the original title of the conference is probably more succinct in its description of the event.

There was once a convention like today.

Where was this convention? It was held in Jerusalem.

Jerusalem is a most holy place, the place where Jesus was crucified. The disciples of the Lord stayed in Jerusalem until they received the Holy Spirit and the gospel message went out from Jerusalem! It was at this point that the disciples took the Word to all the world. When the persecution came they were scattered about the Earth. What the heart is full of will come out of the mouth, and this is what the disciples spoke. Everywhere they testified to what they had seen and heard. Here and there small congregations began to grow. These congregations were incorporated into the large church of the Lord, and active life broke wide open from Jerusalem.

Why did this convention happen?

There were Pharisees among these converts of the Lord's teaching. They wanted to compel their brothers to follow the Mosaic law. This resulted in dissension among the people. So, at this convention of the apostles, the matter was to be settled. Resolutions should be prepared and thereafter dealt with. The converts wrote a document, which they gave as a record of the proceedings of the first conference of the apostles. The disciples had started out small, they stood alone after they were scattered, but each gave testimony to the Word of God, and the Lord blessed it. The result was growing congregations.

In that same spirit we are gathered here today, representatives from all of Siberia. Do we compare ourselves once and now? Do we think about our first convention in this simple, narrow hall? This is a simple beginning, which God has blessed us with. The results of the work have spread widely. He has heard the prayers of our brothers and sisters. He has blessed their contributions! For that reason we respond to the cries for help from our audience and His work has spread abroad!

In the beginning there was a small congregation. Today there are representatives from five large congregations. From here the Lord has heard the cries for help and allows His Word to spread! That is why we are gathered here today. We want to be closer together, near enough to touch one another. Man on man, shoulder on shoulder to carry out the work of the Lord. One carries the load of another! We want to be such carriers and we will be such carriers. The strong will lift up the weak.

God will be among us! And when He leads us today, his presence will give a good beginning, a quick advance, and a blessed conclusion to the conference. Amen.

A prayer for all present! Glbst. 541 v.4.

For some time we have wished that we could gather together and know what work of the Lord is to be done, and together support that work. Finally that day has arrived. Many prayers have been lifted up to God for this day. The fact that brothers from far and near are present today is an answer from God.

(A note—before we began our deliberations, a question arose: should only members of our church be present? Many

Henry writing
his journals
(circa 1917)

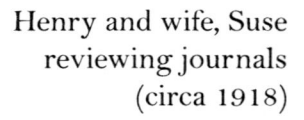

Henry and wife, Suse
reviewing journals
(circa 1918)

Henry Wieler
begins teaching
(circa 1912)

In Russian garb
(circa 1912)

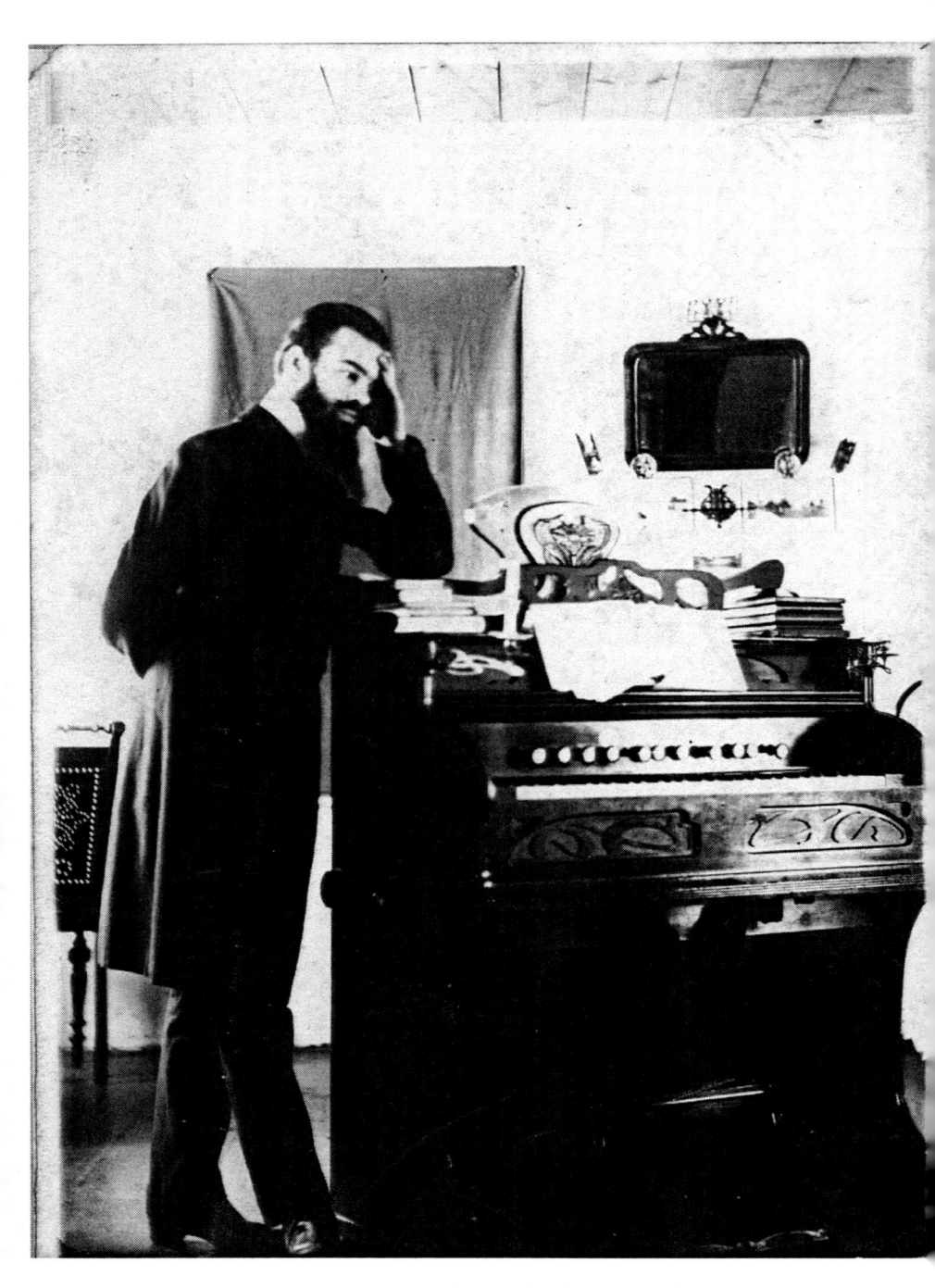

Henry contemplates the harmonium
(circa 1916)

Susanna (Nichols) Wieler
Midwife - Bone setter
(circa 1914)

Weiler's caligraphic talents

Henry and Suse
(circa 1919)

people left. August Sarnach was among them. He is a child of God but has not yet been baptized.

And yet another question was asked before we could begin: Is it really the wish of this conference to come to unanimous agreement? This was affirmed by a show of hands.)

Wieler tediously recorded all discussions in this meeting. The minutes he recorded can be found in Appendix B. The conference created a set of general guidelines for the church and decided to meet again in the spring of 1919.

The Conference Evening Service

March 2, 1918

Today the men's choir made a wonderful contribution to the conference and lifted the spirits of the congregation with their song. The first speaker, Brother Reincke, of Alexandronewsk, began with N1298. Glbst. He read Mark 13:31-37. His sermon went as follows...

Many of you will be wondering exactly why I chose these Biblical passages for today's work. Because the end is near! The time is near, therefore we watch! The believing community is inclined to spiritual sleep and we should be watching.

Our watching has great importance and significance in our spiritual life. We know that when Slawgorods was founded they first built a high tower and appointed a watchman to occupy that tower. The watchman was there to watch for danger. While everyone slept, he stayed alert and watched. This is just like a captain on his ship in the dark of night. While his crew is sleeping, he is watching! If he is sleeping, what use to the soldier is his uniform and arms? We must watch.

We are to watch for the enemy of the soul. The enemy wants to pull us back under the yolk from which Jesus freed us! A concerned Lord cries out to us, "watch!"

Like a roaring lion, the enemy is seeking to swallow us. The enemy does not always come at us as a fierce beast! If we knew how he would come for us, it would be easy to protect ourselves from him. Often he comes disguised as an angel of light; therefore, we must take care to watch!

The host of pilgrims on their way to Zion came into the swamp of despair. They wanted to rest a little and did not watch for the way! This is how it is today; we want to rest! I also experienced the desire to rest; I believed I was too old for the work. Then I read that David was 62 years old when he took over his kingdom! He was older than I am, so I took on the work with renewed vigor.

I would like to tell you about a beautiful sight I once saw. I went into a lovely garden and chanced to see the sunflower. I knew at that moment the flower had been given the correct name. The sunflower directs its bloom toward the sky so that they face the sun directly. The warmth attracts them skyward. Let us be so attracted to the Son of righteousness! At noon, I went to the garden again. Again, the flower had followed the sun's path in the sky. O, that we would also experience this warmth and that we would follow the sun with the eyes of our faith. Watch! We are especially in need of watchfulness.

The enemy did not allow the Son of God to be tempted himself. How much more will he want to work on us? We surely do not deny the Lord. Yet, today there is too much denial. One hardly notices if one is having something to do with a child of God. Watch out for the cunning enemy of your souls! The enemy has many means; one of his devices is to make us proud. Our enemy desires to sit on the throne of God. Watch!

Our life is to be open! God will bring us through. The Lord is there at daybreak. The beauty of the red evening sky is evidence. Watch! Protect your praying. Look to the place where the last sweat of your brow will be wiped, where we long to go from faith to experience. Watch and grow, for a dead substance cannot grow. We must all grow to completeness! Amen.

The men's choir sang, "Master, the winds are howling!" This was followed by a sermon from Brother Seifer.

Hymn N1531, v.1-3. Glbst. Text: Ps.102:12-29.

Zion is to be built! I heard yesterday that we are to ask the Lord for workers! We often ask ourselves, "has the Lord sent me?"

If we live in His grace, the question discharges itself so easily! In recent times, there were so many hindrances to building Zion! The power of darkness is great, but we must remember that it is the Lord who sustains us! There is much to do. How is Zion to be built if we do not pray and watch? There are many who still need to acknowledge that the Lord is Lord!

Amen.

Hymn: 531, v.4,5. Glbst.

A Harvest Sermon

March 3, 1918
    Wonderful weather! We awaited guests but no one came. I had asked for room for horses at three different places, but it now seems unnecessary. Sleigh after sleigh came into the village from morning until night, but no one came to our door. So today, I am again a singular person going to church. Finally, we gave up hope for any visitors and I went to the meeting.
    At the church, five men were busy showing people to their seats. The more time passed the more difficult it became for people to find seats. Every row and corner of the meeting hall was full.
    Finally, the prayer meeting began. During the meeting, I saw Miss Reimer, the midwife, with Mrs. Heinrichs. They are both friends of ours and should be guests in our home. Now nothing could be done about it!
    The prayer meeting was led by Brother Hammer of Trubetzkoj. He took his text from Matthew 3:1-12. For the invocation he had the hymn N1138, v.1,2,5. Glbst.
    John, the forerunner of Christ, preached so powerfully that everyone came to him. Everyone wanted to be saved by the word of God. Even the Pharisees came to him to be baptized. In order to check the people somewhat, John warned the people not to be baptized without first thinking about it. It did not help at all. The people kept coming in big crowds, so he tried a different approach. He directed them to Jesus, who came after him.

"If you come to me without repentance, He has the winnowing shovel in his hand."

We are completely open and exposed before his bright eyes; He sees through us. Today it is no different as crowds stream here and hang up their coat of Christianity! It is for naught! He has the winnowing shovel in his hand! John uses such a suitable picture. It is so understandable for those who work the land. Are you a grain of wheat?

O, how wise and good is the Lord. To do his work, He did not get an angel, he chose the people! He himself has the winnowing shovel in his hand. If we had the winnowing shovel in our hands we might let the wheat grow too high, and many good grains might become chaff. Or, we might throw too low and some of the grain would be wasted. He is an experienced thrower. He does not allow the winnowing shovel out of his hand! This is reason enough to rejoice and to worship!

We thought and still think that all chaff are the godless, and this is not so. Chaff surrounds, protects, and preserves the grains of wheat until they are ripe. O, how precious that we still have chaff on us as did Paul. He asked the Lord to remove the thorn in his flesh. The answer of the Lord was so great, "Let my grace be sufficient for you!"

Thank you God, that there is chaff on you. The chaff you have is the suffering, the cross, the destiny, that you have to carry through the world. Let us pray that the chaff will protect us, until we are all fully ripe.

The leaves on the blade attract the dew, and those leaves are our prayers. Where there are few leaves, there will be lean grain. Many children of God are lean, they have very little necessity to pray, little urge to do anything. May God give us the full consequence!

This one thought is particularly important. It says in the Bible, "And He will sweep his threshing floor." How glorious! Not one grain of wheat is to be lost; He notices each one! We always have the broom ready on the threshing floor! When the troubled clouds come, and rain is threatening, we are concerned to bring in the wheat!

Hammer's sermon

Weiler *continued to record the events of the conference weekend in their entirety. Here he finishes with the sermon of Brother Hammer. The biblical text for this sermon is* Isiath 62:10-12

See, our salvation is coming! That is the central point of the promise for the people of Isreal. The prophet Isaiah experienced it here in a similar way to our experience when we see a mountain range in the distance. From afar we do not yet see individual mountains, just simple, gray elevations. When we get closer and climb the first mountain, a clearer picture unfolds before our eyes. Here, we can distinguish every individual mountain and peak.

Isaiah lived more than 700 years before Christ. From such a distance away, he could not distinguish every individual mountain. He only saw the mountain range in general as a simple elevation. Therefore, he spoke about Christ, his first coming, as well as his second, in a vague manner. He spoke of how Christ would come for the natural nation of Israel as well as for the spiritual Israel.

This promise is not yet fulfilled! The wage and retribution has not yet been paid. The righteous one still suffers in the desert land; the godless one still brags and inflates himself and calls, who is this lord I am to obey? Jerusalem is not yet the city visited either in a natural or spiritual sense. Therefore, she covers herself until the second coming of the Lord!

A sea of questions are placed before it. Stop and gather your thoughts. See, your salvation is coming! The twilight of world history is now here; the dawn of His day is not far off. See! He is near!

What responsibilities does the coming salvation bring with it?

Here it is written: Go through the gate. In order for us to be able to enter, the gate must be open. Through Jesus' death the gates have been opened widely. Go through the gate! Many are calling this out into the world because so many have not entered through the gate of grace. Not all people will come and go through this gate. Many will stay outside. In order for my hands to be clean of your blood even I am calling out today: Go inside!

Before the Lord comes, angels will go out into the world. Remember the two olive trees referred to by Zechariah and John. People will no longer hear the Word. Their hearts will be obdurate like Pharaoh's. They will not repent, and instead harden their hearts.

Hear about the gate of prayer. To all believers the call goes out: "go in!"

Go in through the gate of prayer! When the Savior expired before the eyes of Jerusalem, His veil in the temple was rent in two from top to bottom. This veil has become the holy of holies, into which the high priest has faith. Once a year in order to ask forgiveness for himself and his covenant, this holy of holies is delivered for everyone to see. Each one can see the Ark of the Covenant. We do not need a human mediator! Each individual is his own mediator now that Jesus, the divine mediator, has opened the gate wide. Go in through the gate!

When we shall be there in glory, when we shall flow through the rooms with the throngs of the saved, when we shall wave our palms at the crystal sea, only then will we comprehend fully what a great privilege prayer was. We will realize then what the gate of prayer was. The sun is dipping down towards its setting. The twilight of world history is evident. It has not always been like today and will not always remain so. Therefore, a greater prayer life is necessary. Go in! Go in!

How often has the gospel had to prepare the way in this difficult battle? With how many obstacles has it had to deal with? With how many burdens has it advanced? And today? No obstacles close the way! There is no kingdom where the gospel is kept out. How tightly closed was large China? How dark was the distant Russia? Today they are open! The gospel can be freely carried forth. The gate of missions is open. Go in! Do not put your hands in your lap. Who can guarantee that this freedom will last? Who can guarantee if the gates will not soon be closed again? The gate of grace, the gate of prayer, and the gate of missions are all open.

Prepare the way! Prepare the way! Prepare the way for the people who are wandering in darkness. It is not written: prepare the way for the Lord! We should prepare the way for the people. Prepare the way for the people who are wandering in darkness. In this darkness the heathen do not know where to go. In order to find the heathen we do not have to go to China or Japan, there are enough heathen here. People have a longing to be saved. Ask the people if they want to be lost. Young man, young woman, do you willfully want to be lost? No! No! They want to come, but cannot because of the obstacles which we put in their way. They cannot get over the debris which lies before the narrow gate. We are to be examples in our walk on the way. The people look to us searchingly. We should not budge, neither to the right nor to the left. They will not know from us if we allow ourselves this, if we permit this just once. If we can just once go along with the one thing and not the other! Our walk is to be an example so that they will say, "yes, he lives as it is written and taught in the New Testament; him I will follow!"

Prepare the way! Prepare the way!

The way is not just single footprints. Our life's road is to be well trodden so that no grass can grow on it! However, we are already satisfied when we have left a few footprints behind. Yes, how many times have you walked on the way? Once! Twice! Is it good enough for us if we go to a worship service once on Sunday? Is it good enough if we pray once in a day? Is it good enough if we read the Bible once, at the most twice, during the week? Is it sufficient if we become enthusiastic for our Master once in a while; if we now and then get carried away by a speaker and make a contribution to the missions? Then we gladly point to the fact and say, "Observe! Can you see the footprints? I have walked there!"

Good! But, that is not preparing the way! God said to Abraham, "walk before me and be perfect."

That is preparing the way. Many sit at the calculating machine and calculate their obligations. That is not preparing the way. Prepare the way! Prepare the way! Prepare the way for the people who walk in the darkness!

Many will enter in the narrow gate. But in front of the gate they unload their garbage and leave it there. They do not make right what they have spoiled! In my travels, I have been to many places. I have found warm places where I felt the movement of the Spirit, and where the Lord dwelt in our midst. I have also been to places where I found stones, which had been there for a whole year. Then we do not want to wait for conversion. It is up to us to put away the garbage, the wrangling. Prepare the way! Clean up the garbage, roll the stones out of the way. Prepare the way for the people, so that they will arrive and freely enter the narrow gate. Prepare the way.

Throw up a banner! Before the Lord comes, every nation is to have the gospel preached to them as a testimony to them! Today, there is no nation where the gospel has not been preached! Many think that there is still time until the Lord's coming for all the nations to be converted. That is absolutely not true. To the contrary, all people will not be converted; many will not accept the gospel. It is written: the gospel is to be preached to all nations as a testimony to them. No one can excuse themselves—You, o God, are condemning me now! I did not know about You!

Everyone now knows about Christ, therefore lift up your heads because your salvation is at hand!

Say to the daughter of Zion! In the parable of the ten virgins it was said: at midnight there was a cry, a cry from many. Stand up! Meet the bridegroom! This cry could be made today. The time is here! The Lord is preparing to come. The twilight of this age has begun. Matthew 24 has been fulfilled. Israel, the old nation is moving back to its land as soon as there is peace. The holy land has been occupied and now given to the Israelites, and they are preparing to move in. Christendom, the New Testament Israel, is busier today than ever with the second coming of the Son of Man. Therefore, lift up your heads and aspire to meet Him!
What are the consequences of the coming salvation?

The Lord is letting himself be heard! He speaks and it reverberates to the ends of the earth! There has never been a war like the present one. There has been a seven-year war, a thirty-year war, but never a war like this one. The Lord speaks! For people, everything is natural. Inflation is a natural consequence of war, and so forth. But look at it differently ... through Scripture we know that the Lord is speaking! When streams of blood are flowing, when souls by the tens of thousands go into eternity, when the scholars calculate and say that in the last ten years more earthquakes have occurred that in all the previous years, this is the Lord's serious word. He is coming! He is near!

He is coming and His payment with Him! Payment? Are we looking for payment? Is it for us like for the disciples who asked after every deed: "What will be our payment?" Yes, the Lord pays for every deed. If we want recognition, if we are looking for honor, then we must have payment with it.

Bunyan has a nice tale in his pilgrim's journey. In the house of the evangelist are two boys. They both become healthy young men. One is dissatisfied and wants to have everything. The other is satisfied with whatever is given to him each day. It is the same for us: we want to have everything now, for eternity we leave nothing.

We often compare the life of the godless with the life of the godly! It goes well for the godless on earth, they carry out their plans and everything succeeds for them on earth. However, the righteous are and remain a suppressed people. For us it appears as if all work is useless; it is useless for us to advance the Lord's work! We put our hands in our laps.

You have workers. How do you pay the wages? For example, the day worker, do you go to him after he has worked five minutes and say, "here, take your wages for five minutes of work?"

Or, do you pay him every hour for his hour's work? No, you pay in the evening. When the day is over the worker receives his wage. Dear child of God! Trust in God! When your life's day is over, you have a payment awaiting you. Not sooner! Do not be so mistrusting! The payment is glorious and large.

Nevertheless, before you are paid the work must be done. The crown of life beckons us. But, it does not beckon everyone, it beckons those who have worked. The others may probably be saved, but they will be as those already burned but pulled out to the fire. A Paul will not be given the same status as the thief on the cross. Someone who is converted on his deathbed will not receive the same payment by grace as a faithful worker. The godless probably say it does not pay to be pious. We ourselves often despair and do not know what to do. Look at what the end will bring. See, your salvation is coming! The Lord is about to appear and his payment with Him! Therefore, have courage!

I want to speak of Retaliation. How often do we have the experience that we would like to lay into someone with our fist and have retaliation for what he has done to children of God? It is in our blood to practice vengeance. But the Lord says: vengeance is mine and I will repay! We want blood when we see the godlessness of the people and we do not understand God. There are people who spend their entire lives plaguing and tormenting God's people. Should they die in peace? It leads us to ask—Is God still alive? Does he not notice when a girl in Hamburg throws hay toward heaven and shouts, "There, God, stuff Your mouth with that!"

Yes, God has strong nerves! Often we wish judgment on people as it was done to Korah: the earth opened up and let them be swallowed up. We would gladly let fire fall from heaven as it did for Elijah, so that they would be consumed. But God is still. God stores up. Vengeance is coming! Vengeance is mine! I will repay, says the Lord!

What follows for Zion?

Whether they are Old Testament or New Testament people of God, they will all be called holy people. From Scripture we were already named as such! On that day the world will see it and acknowledge it: they are really a holy people! Even the devil will see it and will have to say, "how nice is their inheritance, so clean, and they are so holy!"

They will be called the redeemed of the Lord! We are redeemed through Christ's blood, born again! The world believes we are a bit crazy and laughs at us!

"How can one know if you are redeemed or not," says a woman and shakes her head over the pious people.

"Who can say here with certainty that he is redeemed," says this man that laughs doubled over at such foolishness.

Only after death will one experience if one is redeemed or not! God alone knows, teaches the pastor and preaches about the presumption and extravagance of the irreligious throngs. There, on that day they will see with wonder: they are the redeemed of the Lord. They will be called the redeemed of the Lord. Israel will see Him, the one whom they pierced, and acknowledge Him as the Messiah. Jerusalem will be a visited city, a city one will not leave.

If only we would be that today! We cannot be it fully here, but there in the fulfillment we will be it completely and whole. Help us Lord in grace to be that.

Amen

Hymn from Glbst. 282, verses 3, 4.

I stayed for communion. When I arrived at home, I found completely unexpected guests. Mrs. Langemann was there with her brother-in-law. Because we had guests, I did not go to Sunday school, which was led today by Brothers Schmidtgall and Braun. We also did not attend the afternoon service, which was led by Brother Tuchs. I visited with Wilhelm; Suse had Miss Reimer in her hat! The rest had gone. After the service was over, they stayed a bit longer.

We had the idea to invite Br. Braun for coffee because Mrs. Langemann's brother-in-law wanted to catch a ride to the Heinrich's. My wife did not want that. For her it was not good enough. Finally she let me go though. In those few minutes we talked about a lot: the diversity of the animal world (especially the chameleon), the nonsensical latest news (that everyone should be shot who has not yet been at the front and is now not going), musical instruments (mandolins compared to chameleons), an experience of preacher Lehmann (he was given room and board at a man's house whose wife did not want to have any visitors and when the wife chided the husband, he moved to the barn for his accommodation), sugar, and many other subjects. The time was short. It was, however, enough for us to get to know each other a little more. We believe he felt at ease with us.

After coffee, all the guests flew apart like bees. By half past four o'clock quiet had returned. In the evening, my wife and I went to the service. Br. Schmidtgall was to be the speaker.

Hymn from Glbst. No203, verses 1,3.

Gospel of John 15:1-8

The grapevine is the nicest plant, it is the choicest fruit. It is a real joy for the viticulturist to walk through his vineyard! I do not know a more suitable picture for Jesus than this. He is the true grapevine. He gave another grapevine which was not as good. God got this tainted vine out of Egypt and planted it in Canaan. That was the nation of Israel! But Jesus is the true grapevine!

What is the grapevine's designation? Whoever gets something knows about it, he knows that a grapevine must be planted and it then has a designation! The viticulturist knows his vines perfectly: this grapevine will bear red, the other white grapes; from this one I await blue ones, from the other black fruit. In order to plant a grapevine, the viticulturist clips a vine from a chosen plant and puts it deep, deep into the soil. So it also goes with Jesus.

He was the beloved Son of the Father in the kingdom of heaven. God tested His Son. Father, Your will be done! He is a vine that had to be transplanted. He was clipped from the Father's heart, from heaven and His glory, and transplanted on earth. The vine is put deep down! The vine was put down from the glory of heaven, from the nearness of the loving Father, from the magnificent surroundings of the seraphim and cherubim.

Is his love not deep? Observe Him on the way to Goglatha. He is carrying his heavy cross, the Son of God, whom legions of angels serve, and He breaks down. The vine is so deeply put down. Observe him hanging on the cross. All our guilt hits Him as a dismal, muddy body of water over his head! He carries not only our sins for He was made for our sins! Should it go deeper? He dies between two murderers a wretched death!

After his death Joseph of Arimathea, a respected person, came to Pilate. Someone else might not have gained an audience, but Joseph was respected. He asked for the body, took it down from the cross and buried him in a grave. Completely into the earth! Into the grave! Covered with a stone! Sealed! Is that deep enough? Is the vine put down deeply enough? Yes, God allowed it to go to the limit. Flesh and blood, which His Son took on, is there no longer. We too are to be put down so deep. Flesh and blood are no longer to be there. Flesh and blood will no longer be together. Are we put down? How deep have you allowed yourself to be put down?

Still this grapevine's designation has not been fulfilled. The vine did not stay in the soil because Jesus arose. Thereby he became a grapevine plant from a single vine. His designation broadened and He produced more vines. When the viticulturist transplants vines, he looks at the eyes on the vine. He knows that the upper ones will produce more vine branches while the lower ones will produce roots. Jesus has completely fulfilled his designation as the true vine! From Him we bear fruit, and that fruit bear more fruit. When we bring in a sheaf we should not yet rejoice, but go out and bring in more, much more fruit. In Gal.5:22 some fruits are mentioned.

Love! Is it there? Do we not often take the position of the eldest son? Much is preached about the lost son but never about his brother. We often take just such an opposite position. He did not bother about his lost brother, and when he finally came home, he did not have a word of love for him. Is there love with us? Love should be there! If it were not there, I would put a question mark on your life of faith. Practice love!

Each vine, which does not bear fruit, He will take away. The viticulturist works in his vineyard. His eyes are practiced eyes. He sees exactly which vines are not bearing fruit. He carries his vine clippers and clips the non-producing vine off in order to throw it into the fire. This is a serious word. The gardener asks for time with an unfruitful tree. He wants to transplant the tree so that it might bear fruit! Here there is no mention of that, no period of grace, and no transplanting. Each vine that does not bear fruit he takes away. It gets the death clip; God clips it free! Do you bear fruit?

Why is there so little fruit? One has, if I might say so, one leg on the grapevine and the other on the soil. Some people are half in Christ, half outside of Christ, and thus outside of the church. Is there any wonder that so much garbage is piled up in front of the narrow gate so that sinners can not enter? Your rejoicing, o soul, is for naught, as long as you have not cleaned up the stones and prepared the way!

Each vine, which bears fruit, He cleanses so that it can bear more fruit. How glorious! In the spring, the viticulturist has a particular job to do in his vineyard in cleansing his vine. He examines each vine and usually cuts off the tips. It goes into the fire because it just hinders growth. We are cleansed through the Word and through the Spirit. They make us attentive of that which sticks to us and could do us harm. Everything useless is broken off. God has means and ways to cleanse. War, sickbed, misfortune, fire, water, expulsion—everything is for His purpose. He cleanses! God cleanses so that we will bear fruit, more fruit, much more fruit!

Amen.

No 282, verse 2. from the hymnbook Glbst.

At his time something happened that was completely unexpected, old Brother Hammer came up!

Witness the fact that he even wants to use me, this poor body!

That is how I feel today. I was already happy that I was left to sit quietly in these days to listen to the words of the wise who had sat at the feet of Gamaliel. From home, I brought a flower bouquet out of the garden of Schaddai in case they should find me and ask me to say something. However, this flower bouquet is not suitable now. When I received a short note from Brother Kruger I quickly went into the garden of Schaddai and took out a simple flower from the flower bed. That one I want to share with you. You have probably been thinking that I began incorrectly because I did not pray! Brothers and sisters, I did pray before, yes, I did pray!

Before I give you my flower bouquet, I would like to tie together the flowers you have already received.

The day before yesterday, in the evening, we heard that we have fellowship with the Father and his Son. We were invited to be workers for the Lord, so that Zion could be built. Yesterday we heard that Zion had to be built.

Let us sing hymn No. 503 the first verse.

Now let us pray!

1 Cor.6:19-20

My eyes and my glasses are not good any more, but this is the bouquet I want to share with you. I do not want to make a long introduction but keep myself briefly to the text. I want to speak about the great price with which we were purchased. The apostle says: You were purchased with a price!

I first want to demonstrate that we have been sold! Then I will speak about the great price with which we were purchased! Thirdly, I will deal with the demands of our buyer: what he wants for His purchase.

Some time ago, I received an invitation to Neudorf. With fear and trembling, I went there. The important people were at Neudorf. These were the wise people who had gained their wisdom at the feet of Gamaliel. I thought to myself, "what should I say to them?"

Nevertheless, I had to go. Well, today I do not have that much fear as then. Still, it seems almost unnecessary to me. What should I say after all we have already heard? Even children offer chickens the small pieces of bread that fall from the table! This is my sermon.

We have been sold! Who has sold us? You can read where in the book of Judges. Judges 2:14: And the anger of the Lord was hot against Israel, and he delivered them into the hands of spoilers that spoiled them, and he sold them into the hands of their enemies round about.

God sold his people! God? Yes, yes, God himself sold his people! Why did he sell them? Should I read to you what Isaiah says about that or will that take too long? Isaiah 50:1: You were sold because of your sin!

The Psalmist almost blamed God, he says in Psalm 44:13, "You sell your people for nothing." That is, God sells his people for nothing, as also Isaiah 52:3 says! God did it then and He still does it today. In reality, God does not sell us; we sell ourselves! Read for yourselves in 1st Kings 21. Elijah speaks to Ahab: . . . He sold himself . . . there was no one who sold himself like Ahab!

The first person to sell himself lived in paradise. Who is to blame if you are lured into sin? Observe the virgin! She gives in to the enticer and sells herself. The enticer similarly sold himself earlier when he thought sinfully. People sell themselves to sin! Once you have sold yourself to sin, you have sold yourself to death, and to hell.

Do you not believe that? In Hosea 13:14 the Lord says: But I will redeem you from hell. If you had not sold yourself to hell this would not be necessary. The old snake, Satan, has dragged you there, whether on a chain or on a silk thread, it makes no difference. I will not explain it any more because I speak to the wise who understand.

There is a great price! Paul said the price was not silver or gold, but is instead precious blood. How much blood from animals has flowed for the sins of people. How much silver and gold has been paid for the redemption of people's souls. The first-born had to be redeemed with silver and gold in Israel. Paul reminded the Corinthians about that. Do you know? God has waited a long time. So many animals: oxen, sheep, goats, cattle had to give up their lives. So much gold had to be paid. Redemption was only possible for a short time. Eternal redemption was not possible.

God holds counsel with His Son:

Do you observe, my Son? Do you see what all has been done?

Father, Your will be done!

Obedient Son of His Father! What he has all had to bear! God's Son became a curse. Is it possible? God's love made it possible. Come with me to the slave market, there two young boys were on offer. An Englishman saw them with beautiful eyes full of tears! The Englishman asked about their price. O, they are expensive, very expensive, was the response. He asked the bound boys, "Do you want to go free?"

"Yes! Yes," was there reply! Now, to make a long story short, you know they both became missionaries. That is how Christ deals with us! Isaiah 1: I have raised children and exalted them!

Are you sad that you have not yet experienced the rays of hope? We read about the singer's automobile. The editor of the paper said that an automobile had been put at the disposal of the Mission. Up above the choir takes its place and sings while below the brothers speak to the people; it is said that people gather in the streets. That is what my Son said; forgive me, the editor!

Well, yes! So it was that we were sold, and we have been purchased.

What does He want for it? He wants you to praise God with your body. Praise God with your belongings.

A preacher was speaking earnestly to a congregation. In the back sat a wealthy man who was loudly groaning. The deacon saw that something was bothering the rich man. He went to him and asked him, "what is the matter?"

"Oh, the sermon is going right to my heart, so that I can do nothing else."

"So, then, give a ruble to mission causes and then it will be easier for you," replied the preacher.

The man went pale! The groaning man would not listen. After a while the deacon approached the man and whispered something in his ear. The man was not to be heard again. Later the preacher asked the deacon, "What did you do?"

He told him the facts!

Praise God with singing! Praise God with prayer! Praise God with your body! Amen!

When I see what I have written here, it occurs to me that it would been better if I had not written anything! I have remembered so little of what I heard! This can only be called a shadow of what the brothers really said. Especially the latter from Brother Hammer!

I was engrossed in his sermon. He is a preacher extraordinaire, and extraordinary preachers we seldom hear. It was such a bright, nice conclusion to the festive day; even the sleeping boys awoke and did not return to slumber. What I have written is so pale, so monotonous. These extraordinary people cannot be copied, most of all not in writing! O God! How powerless we people are!

For the closing the men's choir snag the following songs:
All life flows from You!
Grant, Father, Your blessing!
And again a song is sung to the Lord.

Then Brother Kruger delivered the closing prayer

When I got home from the meeting, my wife was lying completely under the blanket. She believes she had inflammation of the kidneys. She had felt it for some days already, one breast felt as if it was pulling inward. Everything together compelled her to leave the meeting before its conclusion in order to go home and lie down.

So, one comes down from the height of Tabor to the depths of the Kidron Valley!

The Lord did not allow anything bad to happen to our family. Monday Suse felt better. For a few days she felt quite weak. Eventually she was more alive. God is gracious! To Him be the glory!

March 12, 1918

A snowstorm is shaking the windowpanes!

Since Saturday this storm has been raging. I could not even go to the conference that was to be held in Kornejewka.

Mr. Emrich is here with us today. He has told me that there is a mayor's meeting today. We do not know if they will discuss matters concerning my teaching. We thank you, God, that it is You who holds the various minds and thoughts of the people of Hoffnungstal in Your hand! You will direct your plans for us. Give us open eyes to recognize your will, and make us willing to follow. You have been with us so long. You will of course be with us in the future.

Hallelujah!

Lessons from the Lord

During the latter parts of the Winter of 1918 Wieler met harsh resistance from a group of townspeople concerned about his method of teaching. Some parents felt that their children were not learning as well as they should be. Wieler argued the point to the townspeople placing some of the blame on the parent's lack of attention, and on the inattentiveness of the children as well.

He takes time to record general notes about his life but focuses most of his attention on recording the Sunday sermons.

17 March 17, 1918

One can hear serious, important sermons from time to time from inconspicuous people. Today was completely different than usual. For some time now, people have grumbled about only hearing one sermon in the morning. Unexpectedly, we heard two sermons today, one from Jakob Risto and another from Johann Klingenberg. The former had Isaiah 64 as his text. The faded leaf taught him and us through him! He spoke of the faded leaf as an example from nature reflecting the life of people and more over the life of a Christian.

Klingenberg read Luke 17:20-37. His sermon centered on verse 32. Remember! Not only on her ruin, but particularly on her priorities and prerogatives, which she enjoyed. She walked beside a man who was named as a righteous soul. She had the intercession of a friend, Abraham. She had the prerogative to accommodate angels. Angels took her by the hand and led her out. She was on the way to being rescued, already far along the path from ruin. But her heart was not free. One glance back and she was lost. Remember Lot's wife!

At last Wednesday's Bible study, Brother Larnach gave an example I want to remember here in my journal. The text studied was Matth. 7:24-29. He told a story about a building project in Germany.

A multi-story house was being built that only rested on pillars. Between each house the builder erected walls. The pillars were made of steel. Planks were placed around the pillars. Between the planks cement was poured. When the house was finished, the planks were removed and the house collapsed. There was no strength in the cement for the pillars. The house fell and ripped down the building next to it. The homes took a great fall and sustained much damage.

This house illustrates the house of faith. A Christian life can be grounded on a rock, but in its pillars there is too little strength, they have too little cement and some time there may be a fall. It does not lie in the foundation! It remains! And so on...

A notice came announcing that two traveling preachers, D. Janzen and Abr. Patkau, will lead the evening service.

March 24, 1918

This whole week I did not get down to writing. I did write, but not on these pages. My teaching books have separated me from my journals.

I put aside a little money to advance our move back home. We will sell most of our belongings. Recently, we have had much news from home. Father and mother, Bernhard, Tina, Lena, Franz and Nelly have all written to us. Father is keeping his eyes open for positions.

Briefly, I would like to record something about the evening sermons last Sunday. First Brother Janzen got up and read the hymn from Glbst. No282 which we sang as a congregation. For the text he read Phil.3:12ff.

This sermon is about Paul's confession. He was taken hold of by Christ. His effort to be like Christ did not please the Lord. Paul was taken hold of by Christ on the way to Damascus. He is thinking of Jesus' voice on that journey. He held on. He is concerned to always acknowledge Jesus. He was not yet perfect. His confession, our confession!

What was Paul's resolution? Forget what is behind and strive toward the goal, the heavenly calling. Paul's goal is also our goal. Strive toward it, because our walk is in heaven also. Our treasure is Jesus in heaven. He is waiting for you! Walk in heaven!

What was Paul's expectation? From then on we have been waiting for Jesus. Are we still waiting? At their time, the apostles thought He was near. How much more closer is He today? We wait for our walk in heaven. Then we will have fellowship with Him and with each other. Our calling is to be open with Him. Be glorious! We will be out to pasture with the Lamb. We will have no more tears in our eyes. Be something to His glory both here and there. Be like Him! Reign with Him from eternity to eternity.

It is worthwhile! Are we thinking of our calling? Only then we will be blessed. Our children will be converted! If we acknowledge our calling we will walk in heaven!

Amen.

In conjunction, the choir sang the hymn: Follow and trust.

Br. Abr. Patkau began with the hymn from Glbst. No235, verses 1,2,3. For his text he read from Genesis 7:1-17.

It was in those days as it is today: people do not want to allow God's sprit to discipline them. People want to work for a paradise on earth, to live in a paradise-like freedom like Adam and Eve. It was then that only Noah found favor with God. God commanded him, and Noah did everything. Then God locked up! That is the focus of my text for this evening.

God locked up! Today we preach about the ark in 2 Cor.5:19-21. We invite people into our ark. Today, the ark is not locked up. When God locked up, Noah could not get out and the world could not get in. He was sheltered. The apostles felt secure when they wrote, "who will separate us from the love of Christ? What will you do when God withdraws, when His Spirit no longer tries to call you with his enticements, when God locks up?"

Christ's blood was there! You will have to tell yourself: I myself did not want to. He is still waiting today. Behold, I stand before the door and knock! Open up! Only that! Bring nothing! I heard a phrase from a brother about the people left outside. Those eople are leaving His presence and going into an eternal fire. People who worked with Noah on the ark maybe said, "Well, we will climb onto the ark!"

They failed. The cold did them in. Their flesh became feed for the predatory birds of the ark. Many have said foolishly that they will climb aboard when they need to. Many will still call it out! It may be too late. Amen.

March 25, 1918
Today and yesterday was proper thawing weather. The hills of snow around town are going down. Out on the open field there is not that much effect.

Soon after I wrote the above, we had guests at our home.

March 26, 1918
The Sun rises on a clear day, now there will be double thawing of the snow. Yesterday we heard that preacher Lehmann, Braun's father-in-law, died. Many events from his life's journey were talked about.

March 27, 1918
Yesterday evening we got quite a bit of snow. Today the wind wants to blow it away. Now I want to enter something about Sunday in these pages of my journal. If I could take shorthand, then these notes would become more substantial, now they are relatively incomplete.

The prayer meeting was led by Mr. Steinborm. For the invocation, he had us sing from the Hmtkl. No 196. Text was 2 Cor. 5:1-10.

Then Brother Dücks, the conductor from Waldheim stood in front of the congregation.

It pleased me that we are again singing the hymns from our origin. I, too, long for the home away from this earth. I see that there are many of you who also feel this longing. That fact binds us together. Now we want to sing another such hymn from Hmtkl. No228, verses 1-4.

I have never preached; it is not my gift! But God's Word can be read at any time. That is why I accepted to read when I was asked. Rev.21:1-7. This passage is clear and it needs nothing to complement it. It was revealed to John what would be in heaven. What is here we know: misery and distress! Beside the Lord it is different. This word is a comfort to all who are fed up with the crowds of this world. He who sat on the throne said: Behold, I make everything new!

That sounds as if they did not make the world well in the beginning. God created the world through his Son. Was it not then complete? Yes! God saw all he had made, and behold, it was very good! The people were happy on this earth, but they were led astray. Their nice relationship was dimmed. Instead of Adam going out gladly to meet his Creator, He had to call, "Adam, where are you?"

How does it stand with us as God's children? Does God not often have to call us? Does not the spirit of the times dim our relationship with God? Today, people want to make everything new. They want to establish a kingdom of peace. People cannot do that. Only God can do that! Behold, I make everything new.

One knows and speaks a lot about a musical piece entitled The Lost Chord. Discord was complete after the fall of man. There was no more talk about harmony. A chord is the harmonious sound of various notes. God used various means to reestablish the lost chord, but a real harmony cannot be accomplished.

A righteous man lives. He does everything God commands and is rescued from the flood. After Noah, people degenerated again. They began to build a tower whose tip was to reach into heaven. God saw that if he allowed it, they would probably accomplish it. He forfeited their languages. Nice notes sound forth throughout from our human tongues, but again and again discordant notes overbalance. The sound of our languages never reaches a full chord. Behold, I make everything new!

I would like to compare the earth to a musical instrument. It has many strings, and we are those strings. God is sitting with this instrument and tuning. He caught the strings powerfully at the flood. At various times he has tuned them. Once more he will intervene with the strings of the instrument. He is already beginning to tune! Then he will strike the lost chord!

The world says that with man, I have my paradise here on earth. It was the aetheist who told this to me. His paradise is his fruit orchard, and it was too good for him. I however thought, I will not begrudge him this. Others put a pillow under themselves, God is love and so he will not condemn people. Yes, God is love, but He reveals His love through His Son. Everyone is to be saved and arrive at the place where harmony will ring out. God desires that all people should be helped. Pure harmony will sweep through the room in heaven. When we make music here, we always hear discordant notes. In Heaven not even the trained ear of Mozart will hear discordant notes. Behold, I make everything new!

No228, v. 5,6. Choir: There awaits for us a home full of exalted power...

Then Brother Waldheim delivered his address with Matth. 8:1-13.

In this periscope, we see two opposite personalities:

One sick person and one well!
One outcast person and one highly placed!
One a Jew and the other a Gentile!

Two different personalities with one desire; to be helped. The crown of their desire is their faith.

The outcast person says, "Lord, if you want, you can make me pure."

Childlike trust shines forth and Jesus stretches out the hand and heals him. It is that simple, that is how simple the way is for you also.

The second person is a Gentile chieftain. Put a medal on their chest, with all due respect for them, on those I want to receive.

The first medal is pure, human friendliness. It feels very good to hear a word of friendliness full of sympathy spoken in a time of grief. When David once left for battle with 600 men, 200 men stayed back. Later David returned as the victor. How would the two hundred other men feel? They were in fear. David, however, greeted them in a friendly manner. When others suggested that the booty should not be shared with them, David said, "not so, my brothers!"

That is pure human friendliness!

The chieftain does not ask for himself. He also does not ask for his son. He asks on behalf of his servant. Today the worker cries to heaven for his wage. In these days, revenge feels good! Many suffer unjustly, but for many the suffering is just punishment!

I know of a farmer who had eight well fed horses in his barn and made his servant walk on foot to the city when he had broken his arm. This man is no chieftain. The Jews themselves award Him this medal. They say to Jesus, He loves our people! –

The second medal is real Christian humility! Real Christian humility does not grow on the foundation of our hearts. There is deceptive humility. It shows itself when we speak to all people about our sin in order to draw out praise from them. That is deceptive humility.

A woman came to a preacher to complain about his badness. Yes, said the preacher, that fact is true. So! She roared off. True humility is quite different; we are lost creatures. Grace is just what we are; God alone can rescue us!

Jesus answers quite simply: I will come.

But the chieftain replies, I am not worthy for you to come under my roof, even if it appears as if I am a respected person, I am still a poor sinner. That is pure godly humility! I am not worthy to be called your son, said the lost son. By grace I am what I am, says Paul. The chieftain has childlike trust in Jesus, speak a word and my servant will be well. Again, see how the Lord uses such a simple way—a word!

The third star-shaped medal is the one Jesus himself puts on! Such faith I have not found in all of Israel. Many will come who have seldom heard God's Word. You, who have opportunity every Sunday to hear God's Word, will be cast out.

There are three kinds of faith: a hereditary faith, an intuitive faith, and a childlike pure faith of the heart. God grant that we also will wear the star-like medals of this Gentile on our chest!

In the evening, they sent to the pulpit the old Brother Klingenberg. In his slow, calm, and loving way he understands how to speak to the heart and to pray. We heard No 126 from Hmtkl. And he read from Tim. 1:1-6.

In the first verses there is an admonition which we have often neglected: to pray for kings and authorities. Maybe it would be different today if we had interceded more diligently before. Now we have much to catch up on.

The heart of this Word lies in the words: ...who will have all men to be helped!

If people are to be helped, there has to first be a recognition that they really need help. Only then will help be offered. Here someone is offering help who really can help. Many people would often help gladly but cannot with genuine sympathy. Here is someone who can, and He already has made arrangements to help! Joh. 3:16.

Anxiously, before a person recognizes that he needs help, God has already made preparations to help. He loves not only with words but also with deeds. I have come to seek and to save! He gives us not only His Son, but also His Spirit, who can instruct us. He has to first bring us to the point that we acknowledge that we are lost. It is characteristic, as with that Prussian soldier who behaved as such at his enrolment. His behavior was militaristic and his answers no less. When he was asked how it came that he was converted, he answered, "God commanded."

It so happens that people do not lay claim to God's help. God does not notice that, he works on a person's Spirit until the person acknowledges, "I am a lost sinner!" I am myself a wonder. In a village, where no one was enlightened and God's Word was never proclaimed, I was converted! The Spirit convinced me of my situation and I could acknowledge it and turn around.

God gladly helps! He gives you the faith, this godly medal! Just accept it. He will help. He helps not just for the short term, but for eternity! You are to be a citizen of the city with streets made of gold. The help from the Lord leads to a place where there are no more tears, no suffering, no cries, no worries, and no longing!

I view with full submission and astonishment into the sea of His grace!

Notes from the Past

The Winter months of 1918 were particularly hard on Wieler's professional life. Circumstances arose that caused Wieler to question his choice of profession. Teaching had become tiresome to him as he was forced to apply the demands of parents and other townspeople to his curriculum. Ultimately, he decided to give up the profession.

He and his family were again faced with the notion of moving to another town and starting again a new life. During this time of uncertainty, Wieler came across old entries for his journal and decided to enter their contents now rather than have them floating loosely forever.

April 9, 1918

Master Winter wants to show us who he is before he completely says farewell. There is not much frost, but an icy wind is blowing and driving around the snow that fell yesterday. However, mother sun is on her way.

I had had the opportunity to glance through some of my old journals. I found some entries written on loose leaf and would like to enter them into this bound notebook. The content of these notes is important to me. The pages originate from a time when I had quit a teaching position in Neuhoffnung, Old Samara and had just accepted a new position in Siberia.

This entry, I recall, followed a bible study on November 16, 1911:

Ephesians 4:22 – In Luther's translation of the scripture the passage reads, "That ye put off. . . ." In another translation the same passage reads, "That ye have put off. . . ." How are we to understand that? The congregation shared much conversation about this subject. A church member noted that at conversion one puts everything off that he recognizes, and expresses his willingness to do without everything he may later recognize as sin. Many things in life we recognize later as sin and only afterwards put off that sin. Our willingness to do this comes at the time of conversion. The Christian life, therefore, is not a gradual putting off of sin. He who has been converted has put everything off including sin which he has yet to see.

I also recall an address made by Brother Töws on March 18, 1912:

Mathew 5:8 & Ezekial 36:25 – Both of these verses speak of a clean heart. We are to be clean, as it is written, this is of great importance. We await a clean Heaven as our home and the fellowship of clean beings. We await the angels, and the most intimate meeting with a holy, clean God. That is our hope.

God himself cleanses us. It is the work of the Holy Spirit to uncover everything still unclean in our hearts. Not only will the Holy Spirit uncover. No! The Spirit will point to the blood that can cleanse us from sin.

His work on people changes because people are not the same. In nature we notice that every blade of grass is different, so are we as people blades of grass. By their nature, aptitude, and gifts people are different. For one person, the Holy Spirit covers up their weakness, for another person He hides their failures. Would you want to keep Him still?

He wants to cleanse our innermost thoughts. People are through and through contaminated with sin! He wants to cleanse us. He puts before us the Holy Scriptures so that we may examine ourselves against the word of God.

God would like to cleanse you from anger! O, how often the children of God roar in their dealings with the servant or the maid. God wants to cleanse you from anger.

He wants to cleanse you from all uncleanliness. How often are your thoughts bad? Even if your thoughts do not become deeds, you are still in a state of uncleanliness. Tell Him! He will cleanse you.

He wants to cleanse you from dishonesty. Brothers and sisters, it hurts terribly if we are deceived. Our word should be holy to us. Sometimes we let our mouths go so far that we are never trusted again.

God wants to cleanse you from your thirst for revenge. You may never have directly thirsted for revenge against your brother, but deep in your heart you have something for him which is bad—this is the thirst for revenge. God would really like to cleanse you. Do you want him to cleanse you?

He wants to cleanse you from one-sided love. He wants to teach you to also love your enemies.

Let yourself be cleansed from showing off your giving. Brother, give openly! Only let God know what and how much you are giving. Let yourself be cleansed.

God wants to cleanse you from showing off your prayers. O, how many of us strive to pray nicely. But think about it, you do not pray for your benefit, you pray for others. You pray and speak to a pure and Holy God.

He wants to gladly cleanse you from suitable praying. He wants to teach you how you should pray.

You are to be cleansed from greediness. O, how we endeavor to get ahead in this world!

God would like to cleanse you from all undecidedness. Place yourself decidedly at the side of the Lord. Do not carry your clock on both shoulders. God only wants whole servants. Serve just one Lord and serve Him completely.

He wants to cleanse you from the spirit of worry, from the spirit of judgment, from all doubt about God. That is just a tiny part of what his Word contains. He wants to cleanse you from everything. Examine yourselves against Scripture!

God also puts people into our lives, those who can serve as an example to us. From these people we can learn a lot. I once had the opportunity to know a man who read a song in a service that went, "take my life, Jesus. I give it over to you completely!" It went through me like a tremor. He has put himself completely at the disposal of the Lord, and so shall I. That is an example of how God brings us in contact with outstanding people.

God reveals himself from time to time with His power and His holiness. There are encounters with God, when we can see Him in His exalted glory, and we are seen in our uncleanliness. Daniel trembled as God revealed himself. How will we experience it?

Summer 1918

The Last Months in Siberia

T*he Wieler's finally made it out of Siberia. During the spring and summer months of 1918 the family packed and shipped their belongings south to Alexandertal Colony where they planned to make their new home. Between the act of moving and his duties as school teacher, Wieler was left with little time to record entries in his journal. He did manage to keep notes of the events, and once established in Neu-Samara entered the notes post facto.*

Because of the war, travel was hard to arrange. Wieler mentions several times that they had hoped to leave earlier, but the uncertainty of the times kept his family in Hoffnungstal. During this time, he relied on the divine hand of God to direct his family's path.

In May, Suse had a stroke, which she recovered from fully.

On August 8, 1918, he wrote the following insertion into his journal, it is the best introduction to this chapter:

A leap from one page to another goes over nearly three months, but I do not want to fill the three months with silence. Since my journal was packed, I made notes on loose pages. It is now time to enter these notes. Now after two weeks of being here, two weeks filled with the work of getting settled and working on new relationships, I now have some urge to write. After I have entered our last experiences in Siberia I can again begin a new chapter.

Siberia lies behind us and so the chapter on "Siberia" has reached an end.

June 4, 1918

A person plans, God directs.

Finally, summer has come to Siberia. After wild storms, overcast days, and cold nights, it has been fair and warm for three days now. Fresh greenery adorns the forest and meadow. After all the rain we have had recently, this added warmth has caused the greenery to flourish. In nature, new life is emerging which is fresh and pleasing so that the poor human spirit is involuntarily raised up into a higher sphere.

What is the drive of humanity? Humanity brings only death and ruin as this immense war waltzes on. We have for so long witnessed the dreadfulness from far away. It appears that our news sources have reported the situation a lot worse than it was in reality, but often we find that the opposite was also the case.

What the immediate future will bring no one knows.

June 9, 1918

Guests! About as many as is in a bee swarm! They tell us that trains are again moving from Issil-Kulj, tickets are being sold to Ischeljabinsk and from there you can buy a pass to Samara. There was also news that Omsk had fallen yesterday. Who knows if this is all true!

The day before yesterday the secret police were here about the founding of a welfare committee to maintain a self-defense commando unit. The Maximalists are to be punished and destroyed. The men who were here said that the railway on the other side of Ischeljabinsk was not yet free of fighting.

In light of these rumors, it would be advisable for us to wait before leaving on our journey. On the other hand, it might be wise to leave know. What should be done? Again I look up to the Father who knows the best advice for us and who has our concerns in his omniscient and omnipotent hand. How good is it to know that it is He who watches over us and no one else!

This morning I went to the service where Mr. Heinrichs gave the sermon. He spoke of Peter, who was described by the words of John as, "the lamb of God." Peter was a special man, and so too is Mr. Heinrichs.

June 13, 1918
Ascension Day

We still have not left. I was in Issil-Kulj the day before yesterday. The Czechs who occupy the town said it was possible to travel. However, the station master had a telegram that said travel was only possible up to Ischeljabinsk.

Lily is well today. She was sick for a few days, exactly why we are still not sure. She had a high fever, pain in all her limbs, and her throat was swollen. It was probably a cold.

June 27, 1918

A whole month has passed since we had our auction. A whole month and not one step in our journey has been made. There is not even a prospect yet for leaving. How long, Lord, how long?

In the evening I chanced to meet with Brother Pataki in the yard.

"Peace be with you," was his greeting.

We spoke together for some time about the illness of the children of God. He sees the cause as the sin, which weakens a person from all sides before his conversion. It can also happen after conversion, he said. When sin wins, it doubles our weakening; it goes at both the body and the spirit. I listened.

I thought about my life. I have often asked myself, "why is Heaven so walled off?" It seems so far to me. When the thoughts and longings of my heart want to come to the forefront, I grow weak and there is no consoling me. Sin! Sin has broken my wing and I roll on the floor in the dust of my guilt. So I have said to myself often. Seven seals with seven seals! I did not say any of this to Brother Patkau.

Later I met with Brother Siemens, a man with a sharp glance and direct words. His sharpness is shinning love. It took us only a few minutes when we first met to become good friends.

This morning we were sitting on the porch together and spoke of various things. Grandmother Heinrichs was also sitting with us and asked if I had been of the 'older German Christians.' I affirmed this fact. Then Brother Siemens asked me at which position I now stood. I did not entirely understand him.

He asked, "You go from one idea to another. You went from the 'older German Christian' church to the German Christian Brethren church. Are you entirely satisfied now?"

"Not at all!"

"I agree with that," he said. "I am also in that position. I was annoyed with these brethren and I avoided these meetings. I once heard a preacher, who was very monotonous, without any expression and without any emphasis, say the following: The irreconcilability locks us out of heaven!"

He continued, "The proof is in Mathew 5, 'if you do not forgive your brother his sins, your sins will not be forgiven.' Since then, things have been different for me. I am still annoyed with the brothers from time to time, but that verse always comes back to me. If I think unforgiving thoughts about my brothers Heaven is again closed up to me. And so I can forgive!"

I understood. This was the answer to my many questions about why I could not rest happy in God. My sins are, and were, not forgiven because I did not forgive the sins of others. O, God, I want to do it. God, stand by me, I want to belong to you. God, open again my spiritual ears and eyes, first for the admonitions of Your Spirit, and lastly for my tasks.

So, God leads people together and makes them a blessing to each other. Siemens told of another situation that he experienced. He was making a house call and, mistakenly, came to a person who was not a brother. Since they were unacquainted with each other, they only noticed the failing at the end of the visit. They, therefore, did not leave without first praying, and the man was converted!

I would like to note events of the first celebration day, on June 23, 1918. We were in Hoffnungstal at the baptismal service. When we got there, the chapel was already full and we found just enough space for us in the entrance hall.

Brother Krüger made a short invocation to the service with the Word from Ps.118:19-29. The gates of righteousness are open. Many have entered, and now we ask: O, Lord, help us. Grant us success! If each of us should ask in that manner, then we will not miss the blessing.

Then Brother Kirsch led the prayer meeting. For the introduction he read from 1 Thess.5:16,17.

Be joyful always! See that sometimes we are thrust into an environment where joy disappears, even then be joyful always! Pray continually!

Then Brother Hildebrand had the baptismal sermon on Acts 19:1ff. His main theme was the question in verse 2: Did you receive the Holy Spirit before you believed?

The Holy Spirit, who in general is not well known, is the one who brought us together as listeners. He also brought me new ideas. He said among other things the following: The Spirit is the last one to come from heaven. He is everywhere. It is therefore much nicer now than in Jesus' time. Where Jesus was, there was supreme happiness, joy, and health, because he healed all pain. But, everyone who was not present there, had to go without. Now it is different. We are gathered here and feel that the Spirit is in our midst and we are happy. Similarly, children of God are gathered in thousands of places and all are blessed by fellowship in the Spirit. First, there was God. Then came God's Son. He sent the comforter, the Holy Spirit, after he left. When the Spirit is taken from this earth, no one will come with the good news. No one will bring the gospel to the people. Therefore, it is so important, that we follow his exhortations. Sin against the Holy Spirit will not be forgiven. Whoever does not continually follow the Spirit, will be lost; because, after the Spirit is gone, there will be no one to invite one in. It is the Spirit who pulls us. It is the Spirit who warns people about evil. The Spirit opens the eyes of people so they can see their condition. The Spirit directs his look to the cross. The Spirit leads from one clarity to another. Without the Spirit no one will come to Heaven!

After the closing hymn and prayer seven people were to be examined. After that there would be a noon pause followed by Sunday school until two o'clock. After two o'clock the baptism would take place at the watering place. Following the baptism, we will admit the baptized people into the chapel. Afterward we will hold the communion service and then have coffee.

The examination of the candidates was difficult, the ignorance and self-consciousness of the candidates was impeding. One young man spoke in Russian, his confession was that all people feel themselves exalted. The answers we received to our questions did not lack in amusement, one lad, named Nathan, was asked if he was related to the prophet Nathan. In his innocence, the young man replied, "yes." A young woman was asked why she had taken part in a Lutheran service. "I do no know," was her answer. She also did not know what baptism or communion meant.

There was a colorful bustle on the yard during the noon pause. The meal was served in the barn and in the schoolroom.

After I had eaten the noon meal I went to the chapel to observe the Sunday school. The children were divided into seven groups with seven Sunday school teachers keeping them occupied.

Just before two o'clock, I walked down to the pond. A lot of different carriages and pedestrians were already there. Among the spectators was a young man in his student uniform that looked extremely bored.

Soon the tents were up and the baptismal service had begun. The baptismal candidates congregated with one another, already dressed for the occasion, in a group with the Elder Bother Kruger. He was to baptize them.

After the ceremony, I walked back to the chapel with Greta Thielmann. She told me that her friend, Mr. Schroder, was also at the celebration today. He was the young man in the student uniform. Greta, for some time, had kept in contact with Mr. Schroder by letters. When their was opportunity, they met personally. Mr. Heinrichs knew about the relationship and rebuked it; Mr. Schroder was an unbeliever and Greta a member of the church. As a member of the church, she had no right to have such a relationship.

Soon after our break the chapel was filled again. After a brief presentation, Brother Kruger began with the reception. The congregation stood and the baptismal candidates knelt. Brothers Kruger and Haman prayed over each individual two at a time. Ten prayers went out of the mouths of these two elder Brothers, and each prayer had a stamp which was distinguishing and give it a different expression than the previous prayer. The conclusion of each prayer was the blessing: "And the very God of peace sanctify you wholly, and I pray God would your spirit and soul and body be preserved blameless unto the coming of the Lord Jesus Christ. Faithful is he that calleth you, who all will do it."

After the prayers each pair was welcomed into the church of the Lord!

After this reception, the Lord's Supper was celebrated. I did not stay for this celebration. We were served coffee so that we may leave immediately. When Greta and I returned to the carriage in order to start our voyage home, Mr. Schroder was waiting for us. While the horses were hitched up he conversed with Greta and when we left he came along with us. He was staying in Alexandrowka with Mr. Gooshen, the teacher. Since Uncle Heinrich was so strongly opposed to the relationship we did not want to mention to him that Mr. Schroder traveled with us.

After the Heinrich's arrived in town later that evening, I sat with Uncle Heinrich by the door. He shortly and abruptly asked, "How far did Mr. Schroder drive with you?"

Now I had to tell him the whole story. Later in our conversation it came out that Greta's brother-in-law had observed everything and had informed Mr. Heinrich of the situation. Mr. Heinrichs even knew that I had sat with Greta in the rear while Mr. Schroder sat in the front. During the drive, Schroder and I pointed out places of interest along the way.

Now Greta was in a difficult situation. On the second feast day everyone was going to Alexandrowka for another baptismal celebration at the church. Greta wanted to go, but since her father spoke about an appointment with Mr. Schroder, she decided it was best not to go.

When the group returned at noon there was a sudden storm. We heard it only from a distance. From the back room a few sounds carried over into the summer room where I was with company. We heard people trying to persuade Greta into something. Seldom did we hear Greta's voice.

Soon, we heard everything! Mr. Heinrich had given Greta an ultimatum: either she accept Mr. Schröder or break off the relationship entirely. She was to decide by six o'clock this evening. If her decision was firmly the first, she should then pack her things and go with Schroder immediately. Mr. Heinrich assured her that he would see she was excommunicated. With that, the angry father lay down for his noon nap.

We also wanted to rest, but in the kitchen next to our room Mrs. Heinrich was debating with the sobbing Greta and we could not fall asleep. Finally, we agreed that Greta and Schroder must get together in order to make a decision. We wanted to arrange for Greta to come with us to Alexandrowka, during the drive we might be able to persuade her not to leave her family.

Greta was prepared to go and she went to her father to ask permission. After a long time she came back with an answer of 'no', so I went to speak with him. I tried to explain to Mr. Heinrich that without the two meeting, no decision could be made. He did not allow himself to be persuaded. He would not give permission for the drive to Alexandrowka, and yet he would not forbid it either. Greta had defied him for so long that she could act without his permission if she pleased. But, she would not be able to count on him to arrange her wedding or establish herself if she openly disobeyed him. If she were to marry Schröder, he wanted nothing to do with her. Finally, he allowed us to go.

In Alexandrowka we wanted to enlist the help of the midwife, Miss Reimer, and we went to the house where she had her lodging. When we arrived, Miss Reimer and Schroder were harnessing the horses for a journey to the Heinrich's house. Having brought the two together here that trip was now unnecessary. Schroder went with Greta into the forest. Miss Reimer and I followed.

In the forest Miss Reimer and I found a spot where the two could wander back and forth before our watch. We could not hear what they were saying. During this time, I acquainted Miss Reimer on the details of the matter. We agreed that it was our duty to warn this couple about hasty and thoughtless actions, and we wanted to do that with joint advice through mutual discussion. We were prepared to speak to them as they returned, but Schroder wanted to talk to me alone. So I walked with him on the same short path he had walked with Greta, he wanted to know where the matter actually stood. I told him. I explained that Mr. Heinrich felt strongly about his position. As a preacher who had reprimanded others so strongly on this matter, he had to handle his daughter in the same manner. He loved her too much, and if they wanted to get married, they could not be happy. A father's blessing simply builds a home for the children, but a mother's curse would tear it down. Besides, I told him, the differing matters of faith will inevitably become a problem in your family life. I told him that Greta had sinned because of him. She should have never allowed the relationship to come to this point. The best thing to do now, is give up this relationship, no matter how difficult that sounds.

That is approximately what I told him. I have to give him a good word though, considering the situation. He was calm, his discussion was relevant and considerate.

When we had finished we returned to the carriage house. Schroder told me that he had nearly come to a decision. He went with Greta into the Garden. When they finally came out of the garden they were both red from crying. Schroder took me aside and said, "if everything is the way it now seems to be, then I am willing to step back and let the thing go."

I told him that is the best thing to do, and maybe later things could change. With that we left. We felt that the matter was not entirely closed with Greta. I believed, though, that I had done my part.

On the third feast day Schroder left for Omsk.

June 28, 1918

Today, Greta wrote a letter to Schroder and she gave it to me to read. She wrote that she had sinned and that there could be no unity between them as long as he did not want to serve her Lord. The letter said that she found it difficult to let him go but she wanted to serve the Lord more faithfully from now on.

Mr. Heinrich does not believe that she will really let him go. I am also worried about what might happen in the matter. On the basis of human advice and understanding, Greta has acted correctly, if she sticks to her renunciation and does not glance back. God stand by her!

The Journey Home and a Story

After weeks of waiting for good news about travel conditions, the Wieler's decided to simply make a date for departure and stick to it no matter what ill news came to them. Train travel was mired in confusion because of the war and much uncertainty surrounded every turn. Yet, the family met with unbelievably good luck in their travels. Wieler often made acquaintance with important people that helped the family on their way. He describes his luck as being almost too fortunate.

Along their journey they received news that the parent's house was now billeted by "Red soldiers." Mother had to cook for the men and father had to pay a hefty tax, but they were in otherwise good condition. Their journey went smoothly and soon they made their way home.

There were many fears that the parents had for our journey, all could have come to a terrible reality. But our great God had allowed mercy for justice to be given to us and helped us so graciously and wonderfully. We went quickly and unexpectedly through all the difficulties. Everything went well! We had only to travel one week to make it home; this same distance that other travelers pushed around for weeks or months. Everything was from the Lord's hand. He has fought for us wonderfully. To Him the glory, the praise! Amen.

Storm and Change
From "Decent into Hell," an old story with a new edification by Jeremias Gotthelf.

The shape of the Heavens are changing. Today the sun is shining in a dark blue sky, in a soft wind a quiet breeze sways and drifting rays give their friendly light to the reddening earth below. Tomorrow the blue sky will be an immense fold of dark clouds. Hail, snow, and a deluge of rain breaks out of the unfathomable abyss, wild storms whip the rain down to the miserable earth. If no clouds go across the blue sky and the earth glows in the golden sun, each tree branch swells with blossoming hope, and the eyes of a person are drunk with joy and his soul would praise the Lord while his hand would expend the wasteful clouds. His heart would bless the day with hope while his resolution would finally take on the storm and the nice things would be retained under the sky. That is how the Lord would do it. He who leads out of the sun from the rosy dawn, just as a bridegroom out of his tent, the one locked in keeps the wind in his room and whose hand clenches the clouds, calls for change, shows the haste of his praise to the foolish human. He will preach to him in the storm that whatever remains cannot be sought down here. He who created nature will not change nature because what He has done He has done well.

This law of change applies to everything that is under heaven. It applies to everything mentioned or born from the elements; even the human race is subject to Him. This law applies to whoever dreams in longing peace where powers are balance, where everyone's interest is bound in the other person, as occasionally the elements are suspended in balance and appear to be bound to each other forever. If this interest would produce paradise on earth by magic, he would be grossly mistaken because such interests rarely stay ordered. Interests are derived from selfishness, and such selfishness could not endure peace. Interests are endangered, the cramps of need bring them into rebellion, what other brought them, they bring again. The cramps of death through withdrawal of juices, the fury of war arises and lets its flames spray over the earth. That is how it goes.

That is how it went at the end of the eighteenth century. Powerful cramps seized humanity. As a whirlwind whirls the dust, so does war whirl nations into a jumble. The French whirl over the sea into hot Africa. The Russians from their cold and desolate land move into tranquil Italy. As storms drive locusts, the hungry who eat everything that is green, so was a wild cloud of untrousered Frenchmen that lost their way over the Swiss mountains in the midst of the green beautiful land. They lived off this land like the locusts live off the green grass in a field. They were wild characters who climbed up the mountains like mountain goats. They ran into the fire like noble steeds who were trying to be led out of a burning stable. Not a small scrap of cloth a big as a hand did they have on their bodies. Still, they wanted to stuff the entire world into their pockets! They, who had death in all their members, gave a loud rendition of their victorious songs, which resounded about. They were their own people. The world did not understand them and so that is how they understood the world. The Frenchmen needed money for a train, to bite into the world of Egypt. Therefore, they fell into Switzerland like children fall over the eggs in an Easter basket. Then France was a republic and the French called themselves republicans. Switzerland was also a republic and the Swiss were really republicans. That is why the French said they like the Swiss like brothers. But they did not really like the Swiss, they just wanted the eggs. The French have nice words and they know how to make them understood as if they were gold coins. The worst hunting dog or scoundrel knows when to speak as if the most aristocratic Roman or Greek was beside him: Brutus and Plato, Aristotle and Socrates mere swine and treasonable aristocrats simply disguised as prehistoric Jesuits.

That is why they said to the Swiss, "you old louts know nothing about what a republic is, we untrousered Frenchmen want to teach you about it. You have lords, aristocrats, parsons, but no God! That is all nothing and must be put away. See, we are all equal. We are all brothers. No man is worth more than any other man. We want to bring you the real republic, we the great nation, the true people."

That made sense to some. The road ways were made smooth for them. If blood had to be spilled, blood then was not only cheap, but it was considered healthy to have brave bloodletting during such suitable times. They asked the Swiss little of their needs at first, their only concern were the eggs. These eggs they stole with French artistic skill. They took mainly from patriots and patricians, from aristocrats and democrats without discrimination. When the French had all the eggs they went back to their saying, "we are all brothers." Now the Swiss were asked to help stuff the world into their pockets and in turn be granted better eggs.

After the eggs, they then took the children from the Swiss and ran them all over the world. They came upon locked doors and they knocked them down with their hard Swiss heads. When they rushed out of Russia over the Berezina River, the Swiss had to build the bridge for the Russians to run upon. This bridge was a wall that the French hid behind.

That is how it was then. If the French are any different now, or the Swiss still so foolish, only time will tell.

That is how it went then! How does it go today? The beginning of the twentieth century shows that everything is the same as before. Storm and change were not lifted. The whole world rests in a difficult cramp. The fury of the war drives disastrously over the scene in the big world stage. Is it not just as if a whirlwind sweeps through our land now and drives the nations to four winds afar? We see the passage of hungry soldiers as sad, daily reminders of the great work of the princes of this world. This war with the nations, this conflict between parties gives us only robbery and murder. We see trains of their wounded and they triumphantly count up the dead adversaries to weigh the toll. These dead adversaries share the same origin and the same language as their death toll counters. One could count endlessly the rows of the dead. What for? What is all this for? To what goal should all this death lead us? Does all this not happen today in the name of 'equality' and 'brotherhood?' The words of "Descent into Hell" ring true today as it did then.

The drums of war are merciless. They create the whirlwind that tears husbands and brothers away, it whirls the patriarchs into the killing. This whirling into death takes thousands and thousands of men into cold graves, and all of this because of a love for freedom and equality.

Where is one more equal to every other man than in a gloomy, cold grave?

Appendix A

Table of contents with original journal pages

As numbered from the original "old" German-to-English translation

1. 1916
   Take a Moment pgs. 1-6
   Of German Christians, World War I, and the World pgs. 7-14
   Death in Winter pgs. 31-37
2. 1917
   The Relationship of the Human Soul to the Creator pgs. 38-56
   Time for Prayer and Reflection pgs. 59-63
   Thanksgiving Services pgs. 70-75
   Braun's Sermon pgs. 75-78
   Two Sermons pgs. 79-83
   The Coming of the Holidays pgs. 83-100
3. Winter 1918
   Prayers for Health, Friendship and Deliverance pgs. 107-116
   The Siberian Baptists pgs. 116-120
   The Conference Evening Service pgs. 124-125
   A Harvest Sermon pgs. 126-127
   Hammer's Sermon pgs. 128-144
   Lessons from the Lord pgs. 146-155
   Notes from the Past pgs. 162-187
4. Spring 1918
   The Last Months in Siberia pgs. 188-208
   The Journey Home and a Story 224-228

Appendix B

Minutes from the First General Federated Conference of West Siberia

1. Elections.

One chairperson: M.A. Krüger.
One candidate: N. Schmidtgall
Two recording secretaries: L. Krause., A. Risto.

2. Registration of Delegates.

The following churches were represented:
    Neudorf, Semipalatinsk,   by 2 brothers.
    Alexandronewsk, Tatarka,   by 11 brothers.
    Trubetzhof, region from Omsk   by 6 brothers.
    Nadeshdinsk, Turgai,   by 2 brothers.
    Hoffnungstal, Omsk to Petropawlosk,
        by 64 brothers.

    Are the latter all eligible voting delegates? Affirmed by the show of hands.
    Besides:
        Sisters   30 (eligible voters).
        Guests   6
        Total delegates   121

3. Overview of the area.

Neudorf membership	56
Alexandronewsk	620
Trubetzhof	circa 300
Nadeshdinsk	130
Hoffnungstal	circa 300

Total more than 1406 (because in each place there are more members).

[The chairperson warns as a precaution that if we now change to appointing workers. The harvest is ripe, the harvest field big, but the workers are few.]

4. Omsk.

   a. A Mission Field.

Omsk is a mission field without workers. To it belong the stations Solotuchino and Rosowka in Thekalinschen.

   b. Should Omsk become a congregation?

The pros and cons are weighed. Pros: Every enemy who wants to conquer territory first goes to the city.

Schmidtgall: The complaints are loud that there is much work in Omsk but few workers. When the apostles spread the gospel, they first went to the cities. From these they won the surrounding region.

Voices opposed (worried about support)! The question arises later automatically. The enemy first asks himself: do we want to conquer the city! First when he has surveyed the situation, does he weigh ways and means for it.

Therefore: do we want to raise Omsk to the status of a congregation? Yes!

Resolution: Omsk is to be a congregation with stations: Solotuchino, Kosowka, and Kulomsinov. Field of work - the whole surrounding region.

   c. The Worker on this Field.

Br. D. Braun was suggested. (His first name is not Jonathan, as was stated to me on 22 October 1917, but Daniel). He can not accept the position today and requests that another person be suggested in case he has to decline.

Br. J. Fuchs has news that a certain Br. Pintscher in Moscow is looking for a position. He is suggested as an alternative if Br. Braun declines, and will be contacted then. If nothing comes of that, the "joint committee" will decide how to proceed.

d. Our concerns for the preacher in Omsk.

aa. Where will the means come from?

It is debated! Resolution: free gifts will be collected, while the "joint committee" comes up with a long term solution.

bb. Salary. 2,500 Rubles. Free accommodations. The "joint committee" has the right to decide to pay more if necessary!

cc. Accommodations. Will be taken care of by the committee! (Whether it will be repaired, rented, or built!)

5. Preacher's Visits.

It is wished that preachers visit each other at least once a year, i.e. go to each other's congregations. When and how that is to happen is left in the preacher's hands. The most suitable time is probably in the winter. Who pays the expenses?

1. Proposal: The sending congregation takes care of him.
2. Proposal: The receiving congregation pays.
3. Proposal: The money comes from the budget of the joint committee.

After a short debate the following resolution was agreed: The preacher expenses are covered by his sending congregation!
Hymn: N1541, v.5. Glaubensstimme.
Noon Break.
Hymn N1403, v.1,2,3. Glaubensstimme.
Prayer.

The free gifts collected in the morning, designated for Omsk, which were paid today were 3,270 Rubles. Treasurer for the "joint committee" W. Steinborm.

6. Secondary occupations for Deacons.

Are Deacons allowed to be involved in businesses, e.g. a bank, a committee, or comsumer? For and against.

If possible, it should be avoided, because it hinders their work. Each congregation is responsible to decide in individual situations.

7. Divorce.

a. In General. After much discussion the result was that divorce was not allowed. Special situations are to be presented to the conference and handled there.

b. A situation: W. Lang. Br. W. Lang has been separated from his wife for 15 years. She is living in whoredom and wants nothing to do with him. He is living an honorable life. His position now is that he should be married to someone else. Should he be married? "Yes!"

8. Proclamation.

Engaged couples should be announced on three consecutive Sundays and then they can be married. In special situations twice is sufficient.

9. Readmittance of individuals excommunicated.

How does one handle members who, e.g., have been excommunicated twice and again want to be readmitted as members? Or even three times. They should be given a trail period. If three times, maybe one year. Each congregation should decide the time.

Readmitted members should never hold any office, e.g. as preachers, deacons, or conductors.

10. Inactive members.

What should be done with members who, for a year or more, do not take part in missions work, e.g. in giving, praying, other work (driving, etc.)?

Faith without works is dead, therefore such unfruitable fig trees should be dug up. If they do not bring any fruit, then they should be handled as it is stated in God's Word!

11. Sunday School.

The Sunday School teachers are requesting the publication of a manual for the next year. It is thought that the guide will already be available then. There will be a Sunday School teacher's course held in Alexejewka. Time: from 17 - 24 March last year (according to the new calendar). Br. Schmidtgall has been invited to lead this course.

12. Footwashing.

What is our position on footwashing? Can this position be introduced? As a religious custom at communion or as used in a household, service of love? Practiced in closed brotherhood fellowship? What is our position to this?

Vigorous discussion took place over these issues! I am presenting some of the main positions as articulated by some of the greats in the Kingdom of God . . . .

Br. Hammer: Blessed experiences when in the beloved brotherhood fellowship in a home footwashing is practiced. Or when sometimes after a walk the feet are hot and sore, and then one came into a brother's home and he immediately brought out a basin and washed our feet.

Br. Hartmann: emphasized that Jesus said: "an example, I give you!" An example of condension, humility (if after a walk immediately the feet are washed).

Br. Krüger: observes that footwashing in the Middle East is an oriental household right. One walked in sandals. Feet were then washed when guests came. It was service provided by slaves. Jesus showed his disciples that he was doing slave service for them!

Br. Braun: reiterated that an example was a custom of the Middle East. Besides that made the point that Paul does not say one word about it even though he says that his gospel message is, "I have received it from the Lord!" Should he not have proclaimed something about it? No! He proclaimed everything that he received from the Lord, but not a word about footwashing!

Braun states that he has nothing against footwashing. He agrees that when he is tired and came into the house with sore feet he would be very thankful for cold water so that he could wash his own feet!!

Br. Hammer: It is written, you must... But it is not said to do it at communion!

Br. Hartmann: Jesus said on one occasion: What I now do you do not know, but you shall know it later. i.e. My Spirit will teach you everything! Did the Spirit teach the apostles this anywhere?

Br. Fuhrmann: It appears as if the Holy Spirit forgot this one thing! He taught the disciples everything else, but this not!

Br. Schröder: Footwashing was practiced earlier. When three men visited Abraham, he washed their feet. It is a service of love!

(and I personally? I know just one thing: I have experienced some blessed hours by footwashing after communion in Old Samara!)

Therefore not as a religious use after communion but as a household service of love it should be available and introduced.

13. Election of a "Joint Committee."

After much to and fro the following brothers were elected:

M.A. Krüger.
Chr. Littan.
Hammer.
Schmidtgall.
Treasurer: W. Steinborm.
Secretary: F. Fuchs.

14. Next Conference.

    a. When? In the spring of next year.
    b. Where? Not yet determined.

From Hymn N 1404. Glbst. two verses.
Prayer.
Closing.

Epilogue

The journals of Henry P. Wieler have much more to say. Wieler's recordings capture the events in the lives of many Volga-Germans through spiritual verse and true life experience. As historical documents, they serve as a valuable asset. Events were recorded as they happened during the harsh years under Czar Nicholas II. The Russians fought in World War I against the Germans, after which came the Russian Revolution with the Civil War of Communist Reds against the Monarchy Whites.

The eventual Communist victory pressed Henry to write with concern for his family "I must get out."

The events of the family's escape with friends into Poland tell a harrowing tale of capture and threats of deportation back to Russia. Divine salvation came in the form of smallpox.

Rescued by a German national who bribed Polish officials the group was given permission to leave Poland for Germany. In Germany, Henry was instrumental in assisting many Volga Germans obtain proper documentation in order to migrate to foreign countries, mostly in North & Central America.

Henry & his family were able to leave Germany in 1923 when sponsored by a Dunkard, a farmer in Chester County, Pennsylvania, USA.

With anticipated success of this publication, I hope to continue the true Christian saga of the Volga-German Wieler family as they make their way to the USA. It is my intention, with Harry Wieler's permission, to eventually make these primary source materials available for scholarly use both religious & secular.

Thank you for your interest and support through your purchase of this book.

-Arthur L. Pavlatos

ABOUT THE EDITORS:

ARTHUR L. PAVLATOS is a retired Lampeter-Strasburg High School Social Studies teacher living in Lancaster, Pennsylvania, USA. A graduate of Millersville University (Pennsylvania) he holds a B.S. and M.Ed. Social studies. Currently, he enjoys researching historical documents, books, and original art. An Air Force veteran of the 1960's, he enjoys world travel and spending time with his grandchildren.

MICHAEL C. UPTON lives in Amish Country, Pennsylvania, USA. He is a graduate of the University of Maine at Farmington where he earned a B.F.A in Creative Writing under such notable talents as Wes McNair, J. Karl Franson, and Baron Wormser. This is his first book length Historical Non-Fiction work. He is currently working on a collection of original poetry, "The Last Days of Maine: Seasons in Verse."

Further example of Henry's caligraphic talents
as practiced in the U.S.